"*Jesus on Main Street* is an incredible synthesis of a[l] strategies that have been and are now becoming t the US and beyond."

—HUGH HALTER, author of *Bivo: A Modern-Day Guide for Bi-Vocational Saints*

"As a preaching pastor in an executive role, I was thrilled to see the release of *Jesus on Main Street*. David Kresta provides both the theological basis and the practical tools for churches seeking to be faithful to God's call to bring economic justice to communities suffering from historic inequities. This book will be my community-development Bible for years to come."

—BRIAN HERON, Presbyter for Vision and Mission, Presbytery of the Cascades

"David Kresta's work is at the cutting edge of an emerging challenge for the church in the United States. 'How to be "present" in helping human flourishing occur in neighborhoods and communities!' Networks are being built and explorers are mapping fresh trails of being the church in the twenty-first century. David provides helpful framings, language, and resources as we navigate what it means to follow Jesus on Main Street and on every street of our communities."

—STEVE MOORE, Executive Assistant, M. J. Murdock Charitable Trust

"*Jesus on Main Street*, more than an informational book, is a manual for any church, nonprofit, or business that wants to partner up and act on making a positive impact in their community, targeting the root of the problem in many of our cities. As I read the book, words like *relevant, catalyst, cutting edge*, and *infusion* kept echoing in my heart and mind. As a pastor and church planter, I also appreciated the level of importance given to the local church in playing a key role in community economic development (CED)."

—VICTOR R. ALVARIZARES, Casa del Padre/Father's House International, Portland, Oregon

"I've been longing for and dreaming about a book like this. In the world of community development, especially in the church, most books simply provide stories and a limited on-the-ground view. While these are essential, what has been missing is something with more academic punch. Something that moves beyond inspirational stories to the kind of book that I can use in my community-development classroom *and* share with church leaders that I work with on a daily basis. David Kresta's *Jesus on Main Street* is an incredible resource that is not only replete with academic vigor but is also a tool that will assist and inform pastors, church leaders, and community-development practitioners."

—SEAN BENESH, author of *Blueprints for a Just City*

"Many communities and neighborhoods are struggling with unemployment, income inequality, and poor social outcomes. In this important and practical book, David Kresta describes how churches can, and should, get involved in community economic development in order to love our neighbors more deeply and effectively. *Jesus on Main Street* will open your eyes to new possibilities and give you the tools you need to make a real difference in your community."

—MARK ELSDON, author of *We Aren't Broke: Uncovering Hidden Resources for Mission and Ministry*

"David Kresta has written a book I am relying on as a guide in my work for its focus on how people of faith can be involved in community economic development and reengage with the economy and their local communities in response to God's call to care for their neighbors. I have needed a book like this; it helps me tell the story of what I am doing, both to economic-development folks and to fellow Christians—and it helps to create new bridges of possibility."

—KEVIN JONES, cofounder of SOCAP

"Finally, someone has written a book about community economic development and what it has to do with Jesus. No matter how many people count the Bible passages that relate to economy writ large (80 percent at least), lots of people still think that Jesus lives in the privacy of our heart instead of in the markets on Main Street. Jesus lives in both places and does so queerly. Jesus dislikes binaries and likes to bring folks together, which is what David's book, *Jesus on Main Street*, does. It makes a space in the market for Jesus."

—DONNA SCHAPER, Associate Professor of Leadership, Hartford Seminary

"If you are passionate about joining God to change the world, then you know how badly we all need to confront our broken economic systems. David Kresta has created an essential guide to community economic development, naming the crucial pathways you need to get started. As the truly local church continues to pursue the justice and abundance of God, we have an opportunity and obligation to reimagine our economic life from the ground up. This book is an indispensable guide for that future."

—TIM SOERENS, author of *Everywhere You Look: Discovering the Church, Right Where You Are*

"Our communities face extraordinary challenges: increasing inequality, rising poverty rates, unstable economies, climate change, and a raft of other issues. The speed of change is faster than ever, and the social and environmental need is reaching a frightening crescendo. At the same time, churches are aging and declining, and change is slow. David's *Jesus on Main Street* is a much-needed resource for faith communities as they consider this new reality. Not only through story and examples does David ignite imagination, but he gives practical tools to discover economic models that are linked to the ecosystem of love and care in the neighborhood. Reading it will have you imagining new ways of sustainability and flourishing in your local place."

—DAVE HARDER, Cofounder and Principal Consultant,
Parish Properties and Parish Collective Canada

"A timely resource to the Body of Christ and community leaders. Any pastor, church leader, and/or community leader looking for ways to substantially empower his or her people economically must have this book. An easy read with practical, holistic principles and insights for community economic development."

—J. HILARY GBOTOE JR., Presiding Bishop, Kingdom Harvest Ministries

"*Jesus On Main Street* is a genius game plan for churches to literally put their resources where their mouth is. David Kresta's practical and profound approach towards community economic development (CED) illuminates the way for short-term goals to develop long-term results. He provides a timely blueprint to function the way Jesus did—first meeting needs, then changing lives, resulting in fruit that will indeed remain. A must-read!"

—MARC ESTES, Lead Pastor, Mannahouse, Portland, Oregon

"Kresta has written a blueprint for community economic development (CED), which is unlike books about traditional economic development (TED). He lays out the problems *and* the solutions for churches seeking to become a development resource. This is a must-read for anyone considering how to reimagine serving their communities."

—ROCHELLE ANDREWS, Associate Director, Center for Public Theology,
Wesley Theological Seminary

"David Kresta pointedly particularizes a platform from which any congregation can reimagine and realign its role in anchoring capital by empowering increased economic capacity for all within its ecosystem, using context-driven examples from practitioners."

—SUSAN H. BUCKSON, Senior Pastor, Allen Temple AME Church,
Atlanta, Georgia

"David Kresta has compiled the perfect resource for pastors, church leaders, and laity seeking to understand more about community economic development (CED). *Jesus on Main Street* is comprehensive, timely, practical, and dynamic. Don't miss an opportunity to read this informative book that will guide you in planning and implementing a local ecosystem with the love of Christ. This is your go-to book for CED."

—TURHAN L. POTTER SR., Pastor, Whatcoat United Methodist Church,
Dover, Delaware

"David Kresta has penned a wonderful and much-needed resource for those in the faith community. His book is for those who desire to operate in a holistic ministry that models the work of Christ in ways that challenge commonly used approaches rooted in greed and individualism, which are often only self-serving. Kresta's well-researched yet extremely practical material provides a wealth of knowledge to people of faith who decide to answer the call of Christ to be transformative agents for both souls and systems. Church leaders who are looking to faithfully use their institutional resources—inclusive of land and buildings—in manners that empower underrepresented and disadvantaged communities will find this book extremely encouraging."

—HERBERT REYNOLDS DAVIS, Senior Pastor, Nehemiah Church (COGIC)

"I read once that there are more nonprofits than churches in the United States. Doubtless that's true, but if the church is taking a back seat when it comes to fulfilling the commandment to 'help the least of these,' we truly should be rethinking our mission. David Kresta nails it with *Jesus on Main Street*. Great case studies, resources, ideas, and practical tips abound, of course. But the heart of Jesus stepping out into the neighborhood is what drives this book—and this movement. Time to reimagine."

—LISA ALLGOOD, Executive Presbyter, Presbytery of Cincinnati

"David Kresta has offered an invaluable gift to the church today, and it couldn't come at a better time. The pandemic has forced church leaders to question everything that it does, from worship to ministry to building use to financial stewardship. Kresta's challenge to church leaders to rethink their 'business model' through the lens of community economic development is an eye-opener and a game-changing opportunity for those who love their church and their community."

—SAM MARULLO, Professor emeritus of Sociology,
Wesley Theological Seminary

"Timely, well-researched, and eminently practical, David Kresta's *Jesus on Mainstreet* offers churches a field manual for reimagining what local mission can be and do. Heed Kresta's advice and discover how you and your congregation can answer the call to be agents of a just, durable, and prosperous thriving in your community. Drawing from the field of community economic development, these pages are full of paradigm-shifting insights for how Christians can love their neighbors by improving their lives and their livelihoods."

—Josh Yates, Executive Director, Ormond Center, Duke Divinity School

"David Kresta gives us a people-oriented, place-rooted, systems-thinking, community approach to economic development. When enacted with the politics of Jesus and a deep understanding of the principalities and powers, it has the potential to develop a kingdom-aligned ecosystem that can transform our neighborhoods and cities. This book is not for the fainthearted. It's for kingdom-minded disciples who desire to be a sign, instrument, and foretaste of the New Creation."

—J. R. Woodward, author of *Creating a Missional Culture*

Jesus on Main Street

Jesus on Main Street

Good News through Community Economic Development

David E. Kresta

FOREWORD BY
Paul Louis Metzger

CASCADE *Books* · Eugene, Oregon

JESUS ON MAIN STREET
Good News through Community Economic Development

Cascade Books
An Imprint of Wipf and Stock Publishers
199 W. 8th Ave., Suite 3
Eugene, OR 97401

www.wipfandstock.com

PAPERBACK ISBN: 978–1–7252–7516–4
HARDCOVER ISBN: 978–1–7252–7511–9
EBOOK ISBN: 978–1–7252–7515–7

Cataloguing-in-Publication data:

Names: Kresta, David E., author. | Metzger, Paul Louis, foreword.

Title: Jesus on Main Street: Good News through Community Economic Development / David E. Kresta ; with a foreword by Paul Louis Metzger.

Description: Eugene, OR : Cascade Books, 2021 | | Includes bibliographical references.

Identifiers: ISBN 978–1–7252–7516–4 (paperback) | ISBN 978–1–7252–7511–9 (hardcover) | ISBN 978–1–7252–7515–7 (ebook)

Subjects: LCSH: Economics—Religious aspects—Christianity. | Church and social problems. | Local government—United States. | Community development—United States. | Economic development projects—United States.

Classification: BR115.E3 K74 2021 (print) | BR115.E3 K74 (ebook)

Table of Contents

List of Tables

List of Figures

Foreword

THERE'S AN OLD SAYING that goes "Don't be so heavenly minded that you're of no earthly good." Someone can be so focused on heaven that they have no practical bearing on life below in the here and now. Let me assure you that Dr. David E. Kresta's book *Jesus on Main Street* does not fall prey to this critique. To the contrary, Kresta's book is so filled with earthly, practical wisdom that it is of great heavenly good. As the subtitle indicates, one finds within these pages "good news through community economic development."

Dave understands that Jesus lives on Main Street rather than a dead-end road that leads disadvantaged populations nowhere. Jesus identifies with under-resourced neighborhoods and locales that fall prey to debilitating political and economic forces in society at large. *Jesus on Main Street* helps these under-resourced people find a way out, but not from their communities. Rather, this volume's holistic and multi-faceted paradigm for community economic development assists them in revitalizing their communities from the inside out in just and equitable ways. Contrary to Wall Street prophets, who all too often preach big is better, cater to the rich and powerful, and fleece the little flock, we find in this book a modern-day, living example of how Jesus goes quietly about his business on Main Street, guarding against breaking bruised reeds and snuffing out smoldering wicks until he brings justice to the nations (Matt 12:15–21).

David discerns that Jesus has a lot to say about money and the state of our souls. Rather than disregarding money as if it were the root of all evil, he understands that the *love* of money is evil's root (1 Tim 6:10) and that the proper use of it benefits the common good and furthers Jesus' kingdom aims. Rather than thinking that because God has given us the kingdom we do not need to care about the poor, this church handbook for community economic development accounts for Jesus' teaching that we must care for the poor because God has given us the kingdom. The Jesus who shows up on Main Street makes clear:

> Do not be afraid, little flock, for your Father has been pleased to give you the kingdom. Sell your possessions and give to the poor. Provide purses for yourselves that will not wear out, a treasure in heaven that will never fail, where no thief comes near and no moth destroys. For where your treasure is, there your heart will be also. (Luke 12:32–34)

The preceding reflections may or may not sit well with those who think that the "good news" of Jesus is simply about saving individual souls. Of course, the good news of Jesus involves the utmost concern for eternal destiny. But the good news of Jesus' kingdom addresses embodied souls, not disembodied spirits, as in gnostic spirituality. The good news of Jesus' kingdom's emphasis on embodied spirituality also entails spatial and temporal configurations and social realities of various kinds, including economic structures. The Sermon on the Mount with its declaration "Blessed are the poor in spirit" (Matt 5:3), or what John R. W. Stott referred to as "spiritual bankruptcy,"[1] complements well Luke's emphasis on "Blessed are you who are poor" (Luke 6:20) in contrast to the rich whom Jesus curses for their lives of self-absorbed comfort (Luke 6:24). Those who are rich toward God realize how needy they are for God's gift of eternal life. Their sense of need carries over to addressing social inequities. They know that the same Jesus who read from that scroll of Isaiah in the synagogue in his hometown of Nazareth (Luke 4:16–18a), and who lives on Main Street in the United States, was anointed "to proclaim good news to the poor." The Spirit led Jesus "to proclaim freedom for the prisoners and recovery of sight for the blind, to set the oppressed free, to proclaim the year of the Lord's favor" (Luke 4:18b–19). Luke's Gospel gives attention to various structures that weigh down the masses. But Jesus comes to liberate them from their oppression and usher in the ultimate year of Jubilee ("the year of the Lord's favor"; Luke 4:19). Regardless of what you make of the supposed "social gospel," the gospel surely is social rather than anti-social in its import. So, how social will our view of the gospel be today?

All too often, conservative Christians focus on individual, personal relationships and fail to account for social structures.[2] For their part, liberal Christians often focus on social structures and discount the import of

---

1. Stott, *Sermon on the Mount*.
2. Emerson and Smith, *Divided by Faith*.

individual, personal relationships. David's keen sense entails both options. Contrary to those bumper stickers claiming solely that "Jesus is changing one person at a time," David's car bumper reads more like "Jesus is changing one person and one interpersonal structure at a time." This twofold emphasis is certainly evident in Jesus going to Zacchaeus the chief tax collector's house to dine with him. Transformed by Jesus' presence, Zacchaeus repents and believes in the Lord. Zacchaeus' repentance is real in that he is going to make right what he did wrong in cheating others and taking their money (Luke 19:1–10). If we are concerned for the good news of Jesus' upside down and downwardly mobile kingdom and not some privatized and upwardly mobile prosperity gospel, we will take to heart the following:

> But Zacchaeus stood up and said to the Lord, "Look, Lord! Here and now I give half of my possessions to the poor, and if I have cheated anybody out of anything, I will pay back four times the amount." Jesus said to him, "Today salvation has come to this house, because this man, too, is a son of Abraham. For the Son of Man came to seek and to save the lost." (Luke 19:8–10)

If we concern ourselves with reaching those who do not yet know Jesus and whom the dominant forces often put out of reach, we will expand our sense of the power and scope of Jesus' gospel of the inside out and upside down kingdom.

In this book, David brings together his expertise in urban studies and community economic development in pursuit of his vision and passion for holistic gospel and local church witness in service to underrepresented populations. The result is an interdisciplinary resource manual that will help people of all walks of life and traditions work comprehensively, collaboratively, and entrepreneurially to foster vital social ecosystems for the sake of human flourishing in vulnerable local communities. His multifaceted and visionary venture serves as a fitting complement to prior manifestos in Christian community development[3] and recent expositions of theology in a more liberating and justice-centered vein.[4]

Perhaps some of you who are committed to community economic development are looking to foster a network of likeminded individuals and organizations. Still, you are wary of the church. Perhaps you have witnessed some churches operating in a self-serving and dishonoring manner in their communities, or perhaps experienced churches as detached and

3. Perkins, *With Justice for All.*
4. Cannon and Smith, *Evangelical Theologies.*

not engaged at all. David's model of the church and its humble, open, and gracious posture provides a much-needed alternative paradigm. I resonate with his passion for connection and affirmation of those local churches working collaboratively and comprehensively with disadvantaged populations in equitable and dignifying ways close to home and far and wide. He firmly believes churches can be part of the solution rather than a core part of the problem by providing a bolster against larger market and institutional forces. For example, these churches can offer multipurpose space for their surrounding neighborhoods' everyday use for counsel, networking, mentoring, education, and advocacy. Contrary to Jesus on Main Street, Jesus on Wall Street focuses on church growth at the expense of local community engagement, easily leading to the dark side of gentrification and related forces. In contrast, one finds here a guide for how the local church can be salt and light—a preserving and penetrating influence in its surrounding community. The book takes seriously the need for the church to foster a form of discipleship that accounts for local and "global real estate" that deconstructs our racialized world of displacement and disparity in pursuit of equitable and liberating "living arrangements."[5] In addition to finding consideration of merchants and businesses in the pages that follow, *Jesus on Main Street* turns the church as a vendor of religious goods and services[6] or faith-based emporium[7] fixated on profit margins into a creative catalyst pursuing justice for all those on society's margins.

The result of Dr. Kresta's years of painstaking research, practical assessments of various communities, and helpful strategies is a robust and realistic introduction, overview, and roadmap for how churches can go about pursuing and fostering community economic development. Those who take this book to heart will have a far better sense of the strengths, weaknesses, opportunities, and threats to sound practices. This book's navigation system will help those interested in community economic development avoid detours and wrong turns. They will follow Jesus down Main Street to the place where he lives. Come and see.

Paul Louis Metzger, PhD
Professor of Theology & Culture
Multnomah University & Seminary

5. Jennings, *Christian Imagination*.
6. Hunsberger, *Missional Vocation*.
7. Metzger, *Consuming Jesus*.

Introduction

"God loves just economies."

THIS STATEMENT ON ITS own is a perfect introduction to this book. But please allow me to expand a little at the risk of unbalancing this perfection. God's perfect design includes just relationships within just economic systems, explaining why the Bible begins with a perfect, sustainable, rural economy and ends with a perfect, sustainable, urban economy. By taking on the mantle that Jesus took for himself when he announced freedom for the poor and oppressed (Luke 3:18), we have a role to play in helping establish just economies in the here and now.

But why does God love just economies? Because God loves people and that means God loves justice! In *Pursuing Justice*, Ken Wystma explains that justice should be central to the church because it is central to the nature of God and his good news:

> Justice is rooted in the character of God, established in the creation of God, mandated by the commands of God, present in the kingdom of God, motivated by the love of God, affirmed in the teaching of Jesus, reflected in the example of Jesus, and carried on today by all who are moved and led by the Spirit.[1]

God has raised prophets throughout the ages to call attention to injustice, much of it explicit in its critique of economic systems and practices. For example, Ezekiel commanded the use of honest scales and weights (Ezek 45:10) and Malachi railed against wage theft and oppression (Mal 3:5). Jesus preached within an unjust Roman economic system that took advantage of poor farmers and villagers, explaining the prevalence of

---

1. Wytsma, *Pursuing Justice*, xxii.

economic themes in so many of his parables.[2] Although far removed in time and place, our country's current economic system is similarly unjust, with cracks chiseled by the invisible hand of the market as it unsuccessfully tries to provide economic opportunity for all. This book is for you if you know this to be true and want to lead your church in following Jesus into those cracks.

Along with being rooted in God's love and justice, the church occupies a unique position in society, calling for *more* engagement in processes such as economic development. As followers of Jesus, we are called to live and love sacrificially, being above the fray, so to speak, of special interest groups or community constituencies. Luke Bretherton, professor of moral and political theology at Duke Divinity School, cautions against the church falling for the three related temptations of being just another interest group, acting as a collective of individuals preserving their rights, and providing a product to be consumed in the marketplace of lifestyle choices. Churches that fall to these temptations "situate the church in a competitive and conflictual relationship with other groups in society . . . so that instead of seeing others as neighbors to be loved, they emerge as enemies who are to be demonized, defended from, and ultimately defeated."[3] He goes on to describe the importance of orienting the relationship between the church and community around a desire to meet the needs of the entire community, building and maintaining a vision of the common good rather than defending its own interests. Who better to fight for economic justice than local churches uniquely positioned by God to be salt and light in society?

Economic systems span many layers, starting from global flows of capital, to national and state policies and programs, down to local economies, and finally into our closets, garages, and refrigerators. Based on a strong history of church-based social justice that has helped overthrow evil systems such as the Atlantic slave trade and child labor, we certainly shouldn't be afraid to take on big global systems. Indeed, there is excellent faith-based work[4] going on to challenge the current ideology of neoliberal capitalism. However, in this book we've set our sights at the local community level. Why? Because it's on Main Street[5] that the cracks mentioned above

2. Horsley, *You Shall Not Bow Down*.

3. Bretherton, "Religion and the Salvation of Urban Politics," 215.

4. See for example Block et al., *An Other Kingdom*.

5. "Main Street" is typical short-hand for the site of local economic activity, as opposed to "Wall Street," which is emblematic of international, global economic activity and big business.

are most visible, intersecting with the sphere of local churches and thereby providing a tremendous opportunity for the church to bring healing where it is so desperately needed.

Focusing on the community level is even more important in light of the COVID-19 pandemic. While the economic fallout is still evolving, most agree that small, locally oriented businesses and nonprofits, particularly in communities of color, are hardest hit. Community Economic Development (CED) can direct efforts and resources to these points of pain that are being overlooked as government stimulus efforts fail to reach small businesses and as large companies simply shed employees as they wait out the pandemic. Many local economies will be struggling for years to gain back what the pandemic has taken away, opening the door for speculative outside investors and exploitive economic development. At the same time, churches are undergoing challenges that the pandemic has sped up, with questions about financial viability and how to best use buildings and property. Now is the perfect time for *your* church to rethink its relationship to its community and consider your role in bringing about a just local economy.

The field of CED is a sub-field of the better known field of community development that is well represented by people and organizations of faith.[6] CED is also an element of the broader field of Economic Development, or Traditional Economic Development (TED). However, as we'll see in chapter 1, TED is often contributing to the cracks in our communities rather than repairing them. As I worked on my PhD in community and economic development at Portland State University, I was inspired by the CED efforts of community organizers, activists, pastors, scholars, business leaders, and ordinary people who were working diligently to bring healing and opportunity to the people and communities that were stuck in those cracks. Unfortunately, while there are plenty of books for people of faith interested in community development, church leaders interested in CED must slog through academic books and journal articles or piece together a strategy based on isolated case studies. This book seeks to bring the whole field of CED into view for church leaders and church planters. While most of you will not become full-time economic development professionals, this book can help direct your efforts to contribute to the overall thriving of your community, ensuring that they are as effective as possible by plugging into a broader CED strategy.

6. See for example the Christian Community Development Association at www.ccda. org.

Overview of the Book

In part 1 we get an overview of CED, with a description of how TED has failed communities and how CED can help bring healing and thriving (chapter 1). This is followed by a discussion of the CED ecosystem (chapter 2), indicating the vital role of churches working in full collaboration with many other partners with a mutual goal of community thriving.

With part 2, my hope is to expand your thinking about how churches can contribute to just, local economies. For example, how many coffee shops have been started by churches? While such ventures may provide a needed third-space in a marginalized community, their economic impact is likely small. Is this really what your community needs, or are there more impactful efforts you can undertake? In this section of the book, we provide a "toolkit" of strategies that comprise CED, starting with microbusinesses (chapter 3) and makerspaces (chapter 4) offering support for self-employed microentrepreneurs. We expand to slightly larger businesses with a discussion on business incubators (chapter 5) and worker cooperatives (chapter 6) to strengthen locally rooted economies, along with workforce development (chapter 7) and commercial district revitalization (chapter 8). With chapter 9, we look at strategies to increase the supply of "good jobs" that provide adequate living wages and benefits. Next we touch on the broad area of affordable housing and community land trusts (chapter 10) as strategies to strengthen local economies, before concluding part 2 with chapters on leveraging large anchor institutions (chapter 11) and organizing and advocating for accountability in large-scale development (chapter 12).

Each chapter provides a summary overview of the topic, guidance on how to get started, discussion on the special role of churches, and challenges to consider. Short case studies and suggestions for further reading conclude each chapter, recognizing that if you choose to follow any of these specific strategies, you will need additional specialized information and assistance.

Part 3 provides guidance on implementing CED, starting with an extensive assessment and decision making process complete with worksheet templates to guide you and your team (chapter 13). Next, we cover special considerations for gentrifying, declining, suburban, and other unique neighborhood contexts (chapter 14), concluding with CED funding strategies (chapter 15).

The conclusion (chapter 16) provides some final words of encouragement and caution. The appendix delves into the special topic of reimagining or repurposing church properties and buildings, with an overview of this exciting, emerging field that holds great promise for churches interested in significantly blessing their communities.

How to Use This Book

If after reading the foreword and introduction, you're still not sure that churches have any business in CED, then I respectfully suggest you pause reading this book (and hopefully come back!). I recommend you get your church's leadership team together and really grapple with the role of justice in the mission of your church. Ken Wystma's aforementioned book is a good place to start. More work will also be required to break down the false dichotomy of the sacred and the secular that has resulted in what Richard Stearns calls the "hole in our gospel."[7] See chapter 13 for additional recommended resources to fuel this vital first step in the CED planning process. Without a strong commitment to CED rooted in your church's mission, vision, and values, you will not be able to sustain the investment required to see most, if not all, of these CED strategies come to fruition.

I recommend you read part 1 in its entirety to get a firm grasp on what CED is and isn't, and how it may relate to some of the things your church is already doing. It will also help you identify who else you need to be working with and start you on the road to developing a collaborative coalition, something vital to all CED work.

One approach to working through part 2 (the "toolkit") is to read the overview sections of each chapter to get a good sense for the landscape and how the various CED strategies support each other. From there, determine which CED strategies you want to learn more about and do a complete reading of that chapter along with the recommended readings for further exploration. These recommendations include references for more in-depth education, as well as training and implementation support. When you are ready to start planning and making decisions on where to start, read part 3, especially chapter 13 on the CED process. This will help you assess your community and church assets and determine which CED strategies to start with, taking you from ideas and dreaming to actual implementation.

---

7. Stearns, *Hole in Our Gospel.*

CED: Multiplication, Not Addition

Many church planters and church leaders, particularly evangelicals, have been taught to think in terms of multiplying their church's impact rather than being satisfied with an additive impact.[8] For example, church planters can no longer be satisfied with planting a single church, being challenged instead to think about starting a church planting movement of churches planting other churches. Likewise, discipleship and evangelism is not focused on simply discipling individuals, but rather making disciples who make disciples.

This focus on movement building and exponential growth through multiplication rather than addition can be applied to CED. For churches looking to bring healing to their local economies, the road must go well beyond starting a local business, and further even than helping some individuals start new businesses. While these may be valid starting points, the exponential pathway must include building capacity for long-term equitable economic growth, catalyzing a movement of business creation, employment, and job creation that does not leave anybody behind. This is the promise and challenge of CED as we follow Jesus down Main Street and explore what good news for local economies looks like!

---

8. See for example, https://exponential.org/.

PART 1

*Community Economic
Development Overview*

1

What Is Community Economic Development (CED)?

DEPENDING ON YOUR BACKGROUND and experience, economic development may be a far-off concept reserved for specialized professionals working on international poverty alleviation, or closer to home, backroom
wheeling and dealing amidst bankers, politicians, and real estate tycoons.
Although economic development is a very rich and complex field, it nonetheless encompasses simple, everyday concepts such as jobs, savings, mom-
and-pop shops, and big brands. While even a child can understand how
they connect with the economy ("Mommy, can you buy me this?"), few
adults understand the interconnected processes that dictate their response
("No sorry, my hours were cut at work"). Further mystifying economic development is the fact that most of us feel we are subjected *to* the economy,
with positions of influence reserved for billionaire elites.

The importance of Community Economic Development (CED) to
the mission of the church and the holistic health of our communities can
best be seen by looking at why we need CED and comparing it to other
practices and disciplines you may be familiar with. The starting point in
building our definition of CED will be to compare it to more traditional
forms of economic development. At the simplest level, economic *growth* is
associated with increased economic output in the form of production and
consumption, while economic *development* has much broader concerns
revolving around the concept of "capacity." This capacity comprises the
assets and resources available to a neighborhood, city, region, or country
to sustain long-term economic activity. Resiliency, flexibility, and equity
are hallmarks of good economic development. In practice, however, many
Traditional Economic Development (TED) activities are simply focused on

3

stimulating more economic growth, with very little focus on development and even less on equity. Especially here in America, we've been conditioned to have faith in the mysterious invisible hand of the market. If we just stay out of the way and let businesses run unhindered, so the standard neoliberal story goes, everybody will be better off.

So why do we need CED? Because reality tells a very different story.

Three Cracks Addressed by CED

We need CED because there are several large cracks in the myth of the invisible hand providing economic opportunity for all.[1] The first is growing inequality. While it is obvious that some people, as well as some groups, are economic winners, it is equally obvious that some people and groups of people are never quite able to reap the economic benefits that are supposedly there for the taking. The last thirty years have seen increasing economic inequality, reaching levels not seen since before the Great Depression. Renowned economist Joseph Stiglitz chronicles the growing divide in America, noting that in the recession "recovery" year of 2010, the top 1 percent garnered 93 percent of new income created that year.[2] With a recovery like that, who needs a recession? But it hasn't always been like this: the thirty years after World War II saw faster income growth at the bottom than at the top of the income scale. While the reasons for this shift from equitable economic growth to the current situation are complex and varied, the creation of the field of economic development and TED practices centered on business attraction and large-scale development projects are certainly implicated. Why? TED normally does not directly benefit lower-income groups and racial minorities, hoping instead that benefits will eventually trickle down from the rich to the poor. Because this trickle-down is very inefficient and often non-existent, TED contributes directly to increased inequality.

The failure of trickle-down economics is often accompanied with the assumption that the poor are poor because they don't work hard enough to take advantage of opportunities or because they refuse to leave a "culture of poverty." Others believe that inequality is simply unavoidable, misappropriating Jesus' words that "the poor you will always have with you" (Matt

---

1. A full critique of the current state of capitalism is well beyond the scope of this book. For an example of this type of critique, see Collier, *Future of Capitalism*.

2. Stiglitz, *Price of Inequality*, 3.

26:11) to argue against community development and poverty alleviation efforts. Rather than simply accepting poverty and maintaining faith in a dubious "rising tide lifts all boats" philosophy, CED works to explicitly address inequality by focusing on economic development that benefits all people, especially those at the lower rungs of the economic ladder.

This first crack of people-based inequality is intimately related to the second crack: place-based inequality. We are all familiar with reports ranking cities on any number of criteria such as livability, economic vitality, and even a "foodie index." We see rising stars, media darlings, and perennial favorites vying for the top spots while other cities gain notoriety because they are seemingly stuck at the bottom. Inequality at the neighborhood level is rampant as well, with even a casual drive through any metropolitan area revealing tremendous disparity between neighborhoods, particularly in those cities at the top of the "best of" lists. While place-based differences may be visually obvious, the effect of these differences are not always apparent. Social scientists have found that where a person lives has a tremendous impact on their economic prospects. For example, a child growing up in Chicago's western suburbs earns 30 percent more than a child growing up in close-in Chicago neighborhoods *because of effects from where they live.*[3] As a result, CED is not content with success at the aggregate level of a metropolitan area or region, looking instead for economic vitality down to the neighborhood level.

Just as many accept the people-based inequality discussed above, place-based differences are often seen as inevitable, with each metropolitan area, city, or neighborhood responsible to fight for its share of the economic pie. TED embraces this competitive view whole-heartedly, with many dedicated professionals and elected local officials fighting tirelessly on behalf of their cities, battling other locales to attract new businesses promising high-paying jobs and investment. Sadly, the promised level of jobs rarely materializes over time as cities race to the bottom with costly concessions, literally begging businesses to come to them. These new jobs also typically require specialized training and high degrees of education, such that the beneficiaries are often highly qualified newcomers or existing residents who already have good jobs. TED justifies this by noting that existing lower-income residents will benefit through an "employment multiplier" with the creation of jobs in industries such as retail, food service, and domestic care to serve these higher-income newcomers. However, these service

3. Chetty and Hendren, *Impacts of Neighborhoods*, 4.

jobs typically offer low pay, no benefits, and often require considerable commutes because these workers cannot afford to live near the emerging areas of economic opportunity. This second crack of place-based inequality highlights the third and final crack, namely, a political economy tilted against lower-income groups and racial minorities.

By recognizing that political and economic power are intimately related, CED seeks to transform existing power relationships and envisions a society where all can thrive. CED is inherently disruptive to American neoliberalism's undying faith in mobile capital and unregulated global markets, seeking instead to anchor capital in the community. CED recognizes that community vitality extends well beyond what TED and the market provides on its own. Not being content with remotely controlled corporations deigning to grace the community with their presence, CED utilizes community benefits agreements and other forms of accountable development (chapter 12) to hold large-scale corporate developments accountable to their communities. CED also interacts directly with community development efforts to increase the capacity of local residents to participate in economic opportunities through workforce development and advocacy for lower-income and minority workers. Although neither anti-corporate nor anti-capitalist, CED *does* emphasize locally owned enterprises and locally based economies that can withstand corporate pullouts and municipal divestments that have ravaged communities in the past.

By calling out the political nature of our economy, CED looks beyond simple economic growth. Instead, it takes on the much harder task of economic development that not only harnesses the power of the economy but seeks to overcome the three cracks of people-based inequality, place-based inequality, and a tilted political economy. These cracks, manifestations of the brokenness of our world, call for local churches to bring the healing effect of the gospel to the economic systems that surround our communities. While CED can and does exist separately from the church, one of the premises of this book is that CED can be enhanced with the active support of locally rooted people of faith. This work is a vital component of living out the good news in our modern society!

Traditional Economic Development

Although we've referenced Traditional Economic Development (TED) several times above, we have not yet offered a formal definition. Maliza

6

and Feser provide a standard definition from the American Economic Development Council in their textbook, *Understanding Local Economic Development*:

> The process of creating wealth through the mobilization of hu-
> man, financial, capital, physical and natural resources to generate
> marketable goods and services. The economic developer's role is
> to influence the process for the benefit of the community through
> expanding job opportunities and the tax base.[4]

While the first sentence defines success in terms of economic output and business profits, the second sentence only alludes to community benefits that are somehow realized via job opportunities and an expanding tax base. However, we ask "wealth creation" and "job opportunities" for whom? Maliza and Feser note the unresolved conflict in this definition by observing that "wealth creation and jobs/tax base expansion do not necessarily go hand in hand."[5] In other words, wealth creation most often benefits corporate shareholders while the jobs may or may not benefit the local community. The result is that TED often simply ignores equity, focusing on making businesses successful rather than the health of the entire community, leading to a widening of the three cracks discussed above.

Goals of Community Economic Development

In stark contrast, CED seeks to explicitly narrow and heal these cracks. In his CED handbook, Mihailo Temali defines CED by highlighting its two primary goals:

1. Improve the economic situation of local residents and local businesses

2. Enhance the community's quality of life as a whole (appearance, safety, networks, gathering places, sense of positive momentum)[6]

This definition frames CED as place-based and local in nature, centered on equity, with overall community quality of life as the ultimate measure of success rather than the vagaries of "wealth creation" and "expanding job opportunities." While community development (CD) is beyond the scope of this book, CED's emphasis on *existing* residents identifies it clearly as an

4. Malizia and Feser, *Understanding Local Economic Development*, 14.

5. Malizia and Feser, *Understanding Local Economic Development*, 14.

6. Temali, *Community Economic Development Handbook*, 3.

important component of an overall CD strategy. "Community economic development is not a vision of exchanging one group of people with lower incomes for another group of people with higher incomes. It is about assisting an entire community to rise up . . ."[7] This emphasis clearly distinguishes CED from TED because the latter would be perfectly content with an influx of highly paid professionals, achieving increased economic output and an expanded tax base by simply displacing the poor.

The emphasis of CED on locality paves a pathway to economic resilience and local autonomy. This is particularly important as local communities are buffeted by globalization and highly mobile capital, with absentee business owners and shareholders making corporate decisions such as downsizing, corporate relocations, and other profit-seeking actions, with little to no regard for the surrounding communities. Scholar James DeFilippis[8] critiques the current neoliberal economic system underlying such community destruction, pointing out that it is not an economic given but rather a politically and socially constructed system. The answer in his estimation is local autonomy not as an end, but rather a means to transform power relations and improve everybody's life within the community. He frames "alternative" economic structures such as ESOPs (employee stock ownership plans), worker cooperatives, community currencies, and community land trusts as a means to limit the devastating effects of highly mobile capital and globalization. He develops this focus of local autonomy and community ownership into the concept of "economic democracy,"[9] providing a powerful north star to guide CED. By focusing on development that gives people more control of the economic processes and institutions that impact them, communities are not forced into the false dichotomy of economic growth versus healthy and thriving communities for all.

Before concluding this chapter, we will round out our understanding of CED by comparing and contrasting it to a variety of related concepts including bi-vocational church planting, church-launched businesses, community development, business as mission, marketplace ministries, poverty alleviation, and theology of work.

7. Temali, *Community Economic Development Handbook*, 2.

8. DeFilippis, *Unmaking Goliath*.

9. Casper-Futterman and Defilippis, *On Economic Democracy*.

CED and Related Concepts

Bi-vocational Church Planting

While a community that desperately needs CED may also desperately need more churches, CED should not be viewed primarily as a mechanism to plant or sustain a church. The discussion of CED above should make it obvious that its goals and impacts are much larger than any single organization. Nonetheless, a comprehensive understanding of CED can help increase the chances of success for those pursuing "non-traditional" routes such as bi-vocational church planting, or church planting + social entrepreneurship. My friend Sean Benesh is on the forefront of these movements, helping church planters rethink and expand their vision of the gospel in the economic "hinterlands."[10] Pursuing such a route entails viewing your community as a missionary would, deepening your vision for planting a church with a vision for the holistic health of the community that includes the social, economic, environmental, and yes, the spiritual. This could mean starting a new venture such as a nonprofit thrift store that serves to strengthen the community's social fabric, contributes to the local economy, and helps fund church operations. Such church planter/social entrepreneurs can use their knowledge of CED to identify business or nonprofit opportunities that better meet community needs and more effectively connect into the local CED ecosystem. To maximize their impact, church planters could also look to start or contribute to existing CED efforts, focusing on developing community capacity such that new social and business ventures are more likely to thrive, and equipping others to pursue such ventures as well.

Church-Launched Businesses and Social Ventures

With a long history of social service programs, many churches already recognize that their responsibility to the surrounding community extends beyond the physical walls of the church and beyond the "spiritual." However, a common critique of social service programs is that they do not address root causes of poverty nor create long-term change. In the hopes of expanding their impact and seeing long-term sustainable change, some churches are starting businesses or social ventures to generate local jobs, revitalize a

10. Benesh, *New Cartographers.*

depressed commercial district, or create third spaces. Another movement views church-associated businesses as a way to revamp the church financial model to rely less on traditional tithing.[11] All such efforts could very well fit into an overall CED plan and provide real benefits to both the community and the church. As we will see in chapter 2, rather than focusing on the success of a single business venture, the CED ecosystem has the potential to be very broad and deep within a community, functioning to develop the overall capacity of that community to realize economic thriving for all. Starting a church-based venture without tapping into or building a CED ecosystem can significantly lower the church's impact on community thriving and make it much more difficult to sustain the business. In church growth language, it is the difference between traditional church growth methodologies that are additive versus planting and discipleship movements that are multiplicative.

Community Development

As mentioned previously, by focusing on existing residents in specific places, CED is best thought of as a central component of an overall community development strategy. While TED normally focuses on large-scale development with community outreach and engagement viewed as a hurdle to overcome, CED views the community as the ultimate owners of any successful development. CED approaches economic development as a series of long-term, smaller-scale actions designed to improve the community's economic standing *and* strengthen the overall community fabric. The very process of community development, by connecting a variety of local constituencies and institutions, as well as growing and empowering new local organizations, increases the capacity of the community to tackle new CED projects and remain strong and resilient in the face of changing national and global economic tides. While community development is much broader than CED, close engagement with community development efforts is vital to achieving the vision of CED.

11. DeYmaz, *Coming Revolution.*

Business as Mission

Business as mission (BAM) is a movement oriented around the role of business in fulfilling the biblical mandate to preach Jesus in places that are "unreached." Along with the related tentmaking movement, BAM is primarily applied outside of the United States as a tool of global missions. BAM specifically recognizes the intrinsic value of work, calling out the false dichotomy of secular versus sacred ministry.[12] Many tentmakers, by contrast, view their job either as a cover for clandestine mission work or as a necessary evil to fund their "real" mission. Enterprise development is related to BAM, with the goal to assist the world's impoverished via microloans to develop businesses. While some organizations focus on microbusinesses, others help to fund entrepreneurs developing small or medium-sized businesses. Both BAM and enterprise development focus on for-profit business creation, with varying degrees of emphasis on the overall health of a community spanning economic, physical, and spiritual concerns. An area for future research is the application of CED's capacity-building mechanisms to contexts outside of the United States where very different levels of economic prosperity and public infrastructure are seen. BAM and enterprise development, on the other hand, can help inform and improve how churches in the United States engage with their communities. By applying a "missionary's eyes" to their local context, without the at times paternalistic and colonial tendencies of global missions, perhaps more churches here will adopt a holistic view of their mission and seek to contribute to the economic, physical, and spiritual health of their communities.

Marketplace/Workplace Ministries

The marketplace or workplace ministries movement is primarily focused on leaders such as senior executives and business owners, encouraging them to view their business as their ministry and their company as their "flock."[13] Business is seen as full-time ministry, with peer-networks of Christian business leaders supporting each other in the application of Christian principles to build and run a successful business. This mindset can aid in spreading the work of CED as more Christians become aware of the potential alignment between for-profit businesses and the gospel,

12. Johnson and Rundle, *Distinctives and Challenges of Business as Mission.*
13. Johnson and Rundle, *Distinctives and Challenges of Business as Mission.*

along with the realization that work outside of official church and ministry contexts is completely within God's purview. However, while these ministries encourage generosity and empathy towards those less fortunate, these practitioners are typically strong believers in the power of the invisible hand of the market and the "rising tide lifts all boats" myth. As members of the economic establishment benefiting from neoliberal economic policies, many participants are likely to question the critique of the three cracks discussed above, seeing them as either untrue or out of scope for their business interests. An important area for future work is to develop pathways between CED and those currently engaged in marketplace ministries, leveraging their business acumen, network connections, and access to capital to fuel CED work.

Poverty Alleviation

While CED is certainly a powerful tool in the fight against poverty, the goal of CED is much broader than lifting a group of people out of poverty, aiming instead to develop local economies that generate thriving and opportunity for all. The emphasis of most faith-based poverty alleviation efforts in our country are either very short-term focused (e.g., foodbanks and shelters) or oriented around education, training, and mentoring for individuals in poverty. The implicit assumption is that the person is poor because of some deficit in the individual such as lack of skills, lack of discipline, or lack of education. These poverty alleviation efforts are attractive to churches because they are highly relational, but after several years many wonder if they are having any long-term impact. While CED does incorporate workforce training and education, as well as other relational efforts such as entrepreneur mentoring, it also recognizes that exclusive focus on the individual may actually be harmful because it obscures the systems that are producing poverty. Churches interested in alleviating poverty in their communities should be commended and encouraged to integrate their efforts within a healthy CED ecosystem or work towards developing such an ecosystem within their community.

Theology of Work

There is a large literature on the theological importance of work, positioning it as a central component in God's redemptive story as opposed to a "worldly" endeavor associated with God's curse on creation. Work is seen in light of God's call to contribute to a flourishing society, linking our work to God's creative work.[14] In this sense, a robust theology of work can help Christians bridge the Sunday-to-Monday gap[15] and motivate not only CED, but all of the movements highlighted in this chapter. While some writers in this field focus on helping individuals find God-centered meaning in their work, others provide analysis and critique of the economic systems in which we are enveloped. Included in this stream are those espousing libertarian, free-market economic views as the path to fostering God-given human dignity for rich and poor alike,[16] as well as those critiquing the modern economic system centered on scarcity, privatization, and free-market ideology.[17] Works of this latter type bolster the theological grounding for CED by expounding an understanding of the gospel as an agent of healing for all of creation, thereby confronting and healing the three cracks in our economic system discussed above.[18]

Summary

We have now developed a well-rounded picture of CED as an effort to increase community capacity for sustained economic activity that addresses people- and place-based inequality. CED is place-based, focusing on local control of economic processes and structures, leading to increased autonomy, resilience, strengthened social fabric, and healthy, thriving communities for all. CED pays particular attention to low-income and other marginalized groups, recognizing that long-term change will require systemic changes to our political economy.

This vision for CED is certainly a tall order! It should be abundantly clear that CED is much larger than any single organization and that achieving these goals requires a wide variety of skills, roles, and organization types. The next chapter will explore the full extent of a community's CED ecosystem, identifying many potential engagement points for churches to not only participate in CED, but to strengthen and bless the entire process.

14. See for example Crouch, *Culture Making*.
15. See the Denver Institute for Faith and Work at https://denverinstitute.org/ for an organization dedicated to bridging the gap often found between faith and work.
16. Bolt, *Economic Shalom*.
17. Block et al., *Other Kingdom*.
18. See also https://www.theologyofwork.org/ and https://oikonomianetwork.org/.

2

The CED Ecosystem and the Role of Local Churches

Overview

OUR CURRENT ECONOMIC SYSTEM is complex, comprising multiple actors with conflicting requirements that combine to continually disadvantage the marginalized. Likewise, bringing healing and enhancing a local community's quality of life is complex, requiring a high degree of collaboration between constituents as varied as business owners, banks, corporations, churches, local government agencies, community organizations, foundations, and of course, community residents. The good news is that people of faith can bring many skills and play a variety of roles in this complex system. While church leaders are not likely to become full-time economic developers, understanding how specific roles and actions fit into an overall CED strategy is important in order to use precious church resources as efficiently as possible and maximize a church's contribution to community thriving. Understanding the full picture of CED can also highlight gaps or blind spots that could hinder thriving, especially among the marginalized and forgotten segments of society—the very people Jesus sought out!

Decentering the Church

CED is a highly collaborative endeavor, calling for a *decentered* church posture. If the church is not at the center of CED, then who or what is? We submit that the *community*, with its various constituents and stakeholders, is the proper focus for CED, with the church as a member of a larger CED

14

ecosystem contributing to community thriving. This may be particularly difficult for churches and leaders who are used to being in the driver's seat and may worry about diluting the church's impact or compromising the church's values. However, a central premise of this book is that churches can *expand* their impact on community thriving via CED, recalling our distinction between multiplicative and additive impacts from the introduction. As discussed in chapter 1 and again in chapter 13, we also stress the importance of clarifying and solidifying your church's mission, vision, and values to provide ongoing guidance and protection against concerns about compromise that may arise in a heavily collaborative process.

Rather than centering on the interests of a specific organization or constituency, the focus and challenge of CED is to build and activate a local ecosystem with a common vision of community thriving through a just, local economy. While these first two chapters reveal that CED is a large undertaking, our intention is not to discourage or overwhelm you. Rather, as this complex ecosystem is described below, we hope that you will consider how you as a church leader or church planter, your church as a community actor, and the individuals within your church, can best fit into this CED ecosystem. You may be the right person or organization to take on a central role such as ecosystem builder or facilitator. Or you may choose to fill a more specialized role, for example, as an organizer working with a marginalized group, an entrepreneur providing a specific community need, or as a provider of space for businesses and nonprofits.

The details of planning and implementing CED will be addressed in part 3 of this book; here we focus on unpacking the CED ecosystem and introducing the options this provides for active church participation. The discussion will begin with three approaches or "pathways to change" for CED: development, community organizing, and policy and planning interventions. Four potential tasks or roles for individuals and organizations in the CED ecosystem are then discussed: participants, consultants, enablers, and organizers. Next, we provide a description of the strengths and biases of a variety of sectors that comprise the CED ecosystem and how churches can engage with these sectors: Private Business, Developers, Community Organizations, and Government.[1] Looking at this miasma of approaches, roles, and sectors within CED will emphasize the absolute necessity of a collaborative approach driven by a strong, common vision. Throughout, we

1. An important sector in the ecosystem, the financial sector, will be discussed in chapter 15

will highlight the many ways that churches can contribute to CED, providing a broad view before we dig deeper into specific CED strategies in part 2 of this book.

Three Approaches to CED

Robert Giloth, VP for Economic Opportunity at the Annie E. Casey Foundation, in describing the messiness of CED, identifies three necessary approaches or pathways to create lasting change: development, community organizing, and policy and planning intervention.[2] The first pathway, development, focuses on the marketplace with business, real estate, human capital, and financial activities. Such organizations build things such as affordable housing or makerspaces, or deliver programs such as workforce development. The second pathway, community organizing, energizes and funnels community power to change behaviors of local institutions such as banks, developers, governments, and businesses. Policy and planning intervention, the final pathway, looks to change the overall environment within which CED takes place, addressing legislative concerns and the overall political economy. A fully formed, dynamic CED plan will recognize the importance of all three of these approaches over time. Because these approaches require dramatically different skills, passions, and organizational structures, it is unlikely that any one organization or individual can fulfill more than one. Ideally, the local CED ecosystem will incorporate individuals and organizations to adequately cover all of these specializations, allowing for various leaders to emerge as the community context evolves.

The Role of Churches

Churches can take on any of these three approaches, subject to community needs as well as church skills, interests, and history. For example, some churches may have a strong track record of organizing their community in efforts such as voter registration or as advocates for or against the actions of local or state government. Others are no strangers to state capitols where they seek to influence legislation and other types of policy. The comfort spot for most churches, however, will be to develop and deliver programs that directly influence church and community members.

2. Giloth, *Jobs, Wealth, or Place.*

CED Roles: Consultant, Enabler, Organizer, Participant

In *Planning Local Economic Development*, the authors identify three types of roles for an economic development practitioner: the consultant, enabler, and community organizer.[3] We expand on Leigh and Blakely to highlight not only economic development practitioner roles, but roles within the CED ecosystem:

1. *The consultant*: an individual or organization with specialized knowledge and expertise to contribute to specific CED programs. Examples include a financing expert, a structural engineering firm, or a political lobbyist.

2. *The enabler*: focuses on making connections, bringing together resources for projects, and building the long-term capacity of the CED ecosystem. As a facilitator and catalyst, enablers will likely not be experts in any one thing, but focus on motivating individuals and institutions both inside and outside of the community to become active supporters of CED efforts.

3. *The organizer*: builds a "voice" for the community, ensuring that no groups are left out or marginalized. This role corresponds to Giloth's community organizing approach above, with an emphasis on building community power so that other sources of power impinging on a community such as corporations, government, and other communities can be met as equals.

4. To Leigh and Blakely's three roles, we add a fourth: *the participant*. Here a "participant" contributes directly to the local economy, for example, as an entrepreneur starting a new for-profit business or a nonprofit community center. Often, a participant does not necessarily even realize they are part of a CED strategy, operating both as a contributor to the local economy as well as a beneficiary of CED programs such as workforce training, business incubator services, or microbusiness support.

---

3. Leigh and Blakely, *Planning Local Economic Development*, 110.

The Role of Churches

While most pastors are likely to be enablers and organizers, some may be participants if they choose to directly start a business venture, as in bi-vocational church planting described above. In rare cases a pastor may be a consultant with specialized knowledge from a previous career, and many churches are likely filled with individuals who could participate in CED as consultants. Church attendees may also fill a CED participant role, particularly those with prior entrepreneurial business or nonprofit experience. Especially in large churches, there are also likely to be many attendees who can serve as enabler-connectors, with personal and professional connections to local institutions, funding sources, government officials, and more.

Sectors Within the CED Ecosystem and the Role of Churches

Private Business

Successful businesses are the cornerstone of a healthy, local economy. They provide jobs, produce wealth, and can bring needed capital into a community. However, a common misconception is that economic development is exclusively about the business community. Starting a small business, improving the community's business environment, or running a sizeable business that employees hundreds of local residents, are all laudable and potentially beneficial activities for the overall community. But they are only a piece of the puzzle. As described in the previous chapter, because TED typically focuses efforts on attracting businesses and making businesses successful, this leaves little time to actually focus on economic *development* and overall community quality of life. For example, many people have heard of a "Chamber of Commerce" without understanding exactly what one is and what they do. As described by the Association of Chamber of Commerce Executives (ACCE),[4] these ubiquitous, mostly private organizations are first and foremost a group of businesses gathered for the interests of the *business* community. This is not necessarily bad, but it is important to understand the strengths and biases that the private business community will bring to CED.

4. See https://secure.acce.org/about/chambers-of-commerce/ for more information.

Of course, private business is an important constituency because this is where the vision of community thriving will run up against the realities of finances and economics. CED absolutely needs entrepreneurs and business leaders who care about their local communities, particularly those committed to the concept of "people over capital." Such individuals work creatively and tirelessly to develop businesses that are profitable *and* contribute to community thriving. However, we must also recognize that many within this sector are biased towards neoliberal economics, disparaging efforts to direct the economy as "social engineering" or "socialism" and challenging the need to explicitly address inequality. Further, because investments in business are done on a relatively short time frame, this constituency typically cannot afford to wait for communities to turn around before achieving business success and will therefore tend to push for short-term gains. Social entrepreneurship represents a departure from this short-term focus, bringing together business acumen and longer-term time horizons to create businesses for community thriving. Newer forms of incorporation, such as the B Corporation,[5] as well as older forms such as worker cooperatives and employee-owned businesses (chapter 6), join social entrepreneurs on the forefront of a movement to reclaim capitalism for good.

The Role of Churches

Churches can participate in this critical CED sector by directly starting new businesses[6] to fill unmet community needs, catalyze a flagging commercial business district (chapter 8), or strengthen locally rooted economies (chapter 6). Churches can influence attendees who are business owners and entrepreneurs through theology of work and social justice teaching. Attendees can be encouraged to approach business as a blessing to the community, with a focus on helping those who are not reaping the benefits of our current system, for example by providing living wages and practicing diverse hiring and promotion practices. Churches can pursue one of the many CED strategies highlighted in part 2 of this book to encourage

---

5. "A certified B Corporation is a company that has met high standards of verified social and environmental performance, public transparency, and legal accountability to create value for both shareholders and society . . ." See Kassoy et al., "Impact Governance and Management," 3.

6. Be sure to speak with a tax accountant and attorney to fully understand the tax and legal implications for your church as a nonprofit institution.

microbusiness (chapter 3) and small business formation (chapter 5), provide workforce development to promote job procurement, retention, and promotion (chapter 7), or enable a local maker movement (chapter 4). Finally, as described in the appendix, churches can provide valuable building or property space for business operations, market space to connect with local consumers, and other creative uses of church space to help local businesses launch and thrive.

Developers

Developers can be thought of as a subset of the private business sector, focusing on the built environment with real estate, building renovation, and new construction projects. This segment exhibits many of the same strengths and biases as private business discussed above. Developers are vital to CED because of their abilities in deal making, bringing together various sources of capital and diverse constituents to make new projects a reality. Because of the size of development projects and the long-term financial horizons, developers are particularly interested in overall community health as this will significantly impact the financial viability of a project. However, even a cursory examination of urban history reveals a saga of widespread destruction and displacement of marginalized communities from development projects usually couched in terms such as "renewal" or "neighborhood improvement." Thus, more nonprofit developers, as well as for-profit developers committed to equity and responsible development, are needed in order to create projects that will directly benefit low-income, marginalized communities.

The Role of Churches

Churches are not likely to play a direct role in CED as developers, although they may have individuals within their church who can contribute as development consultants for church CED projects. In most cases, churches will need to vet developers as potential partners and work with those who are willing to craft development projects that align with the church's mission, vision, and values. Churches in a local community can work together to share best practices and make referrals for developers with whom they have had successful engagements.

Churches power for the fight

Churches can guide the work of developers in their community through mechanisms such as community benefits agreements (chapter 12) to ensure that the entire community, particularly the marginalized, benefit from large-scale development. Churches can also draw attention to and advocate for needed policy and planning changes, for example inclusionary zoning and land-use policies enabling affordable-housing construction on properties previously excluded from consideration.

Community Organizations

Community development corporations (CDCs) have taken a central role in community development since their inception over fifty years ago. Although CDCs have increasingly focused on development activities such as affordable housing and economic development, they also play critical roles in community organizing and advocacy. If a community is lucky enough to have a strong CDC, it should be tapped to play a central role in CED, drawing on its organizational capacities including human resources and connections to both community and government. However, other types of community organizations (COs) such as faith communities, immigrant organizations, and neighborhood associations also play important roles in the CED ecosystem. These COs represent important connections to community members, with vital roles in bringing under-represented voices into the CED process.

The Role of Churches

Many churches have historically played critical roles as hubs for community organizing, including many CDCs being either explicitly faith-based or started by a faith-based coalition. Churches already involved in community development will be well positioned to dive deeper into community well-being through CED. For churches considering CED who are not already involved in other types of community development efforts, we highly recommend building a strong partnership with one or several COs in your community as they will be key partners for your CED efforts. The Christian Community Development Association (CCDA)[7] is a major player in faith-based community development efforts and a key resource for churches

7. www.ccda.org.

interested in connecting with other faith-based groups that are similarly interested in community thriving.

Government

A CED plan must leverage local government for maximum impact. While many cities have economic development agencies, these organizations typically espouse TED principles and may view CED-oriented efforts with suspicion. In these cases, a CED plan must pursue accountable development strategies (chapter 12) to ensure that large, municipal-level development projects accrue benefits to all segments of the community, particularly the vulnerable and marginalized. For communities without an economic development agency, CED leaders should nevertheless seek to engage and enlist support from elected officials and local government agencies. These connections can be critical to overcoming local barriers such as zoning or permitting, as well as provide sources of potential development funds. In some communities, local governments will be willing to lease out underutilized land or buildings for nominal amounts in exchange for a commitment to develop and utilize the community asset as a component of a CED strategy.

The Role of Churches

A mentioned above, churches have historically been at the center of many community efforts to address injustice, whether at the local, state, or national levels. Taking one of Giloth's CED approaches such as community organizing or policy and planning intervention is necessary in order to adequately engage with the government sector and is certainly a role that churches should seriously consider. However, it is beyond the scope of this book to explore these approaches, relying instead of the work of others much better equipped than this author to address this important area.[8]

Summary

As we proceed through this book, we will see examples of the power and promise of CED as CED ecosystems are developed and activated. We trust

8. See for example Salvatierra and Heltzel, *Faith-Rooted Organizing.*

that this chapter has highlighted for you the many ways that churches can engage in CED from a collaborative, decentered posture. The many types of roles as well as the wide array of actors involved in CED is exhilarating, if not a bit overwhelming! With part 1, we've now laid the basic groundwork for understanding what CED is, how it contributes to community thriving, and how the various components of the CED ecosystem are all necessary for success. Now as we turn to part 2, we look at specific strategies that comprise the CED toolkit, exploring how CED programs can deliver good news for local economies!

PART 2

Community Economic Development Toolkit

3

Microbusinesses

Overview

MANY PEOPLE ASSOCIATE MICROBUSINESSES with international development work to aid countries in extreme poverty. Indeed, Muhammad Yunus won a Nobel Peace Prize in 2006 for his innovations that launched the microfinance revolution around the globe, landing "microbusiness" and "microfinance" onto front pages and into popular consciousness. However, microbusinesses, typically defined as very small businesses with less than $100,000 in annual revenues and fewer than five employees, are also a formidable force in the United States. The Association for Enterprise Opportunity reports that an astounding 92 percent of all businesses in the United States are microbusinesses, with these 25.5 million businesses generating over 41 million jobs in 2011. The owner works full time in 30 percent of microbusinesses, with less than $50,000 in annual sales.[1]

The Community Economic Development Handbook identifies microbusiness development as one of the top four CED strategies for economic impact in low-income communities.[2] Mihailo Temali notes the many benefits of a microbusiness strategy, including: (1) a significant number of microbusinesses likely *already* exist in your neighborhood, (2) they are likely to hire fellow community residents, and (3) they don't need to be convinced to locate into your community. As locally owned businesses,

---

1. See *Bigger Than You Think*.

2. Temali, *Community Economic Development Handbook*. Those interested in pursuing a microbusiness strategy should review Temali's chapter 5.

microbusinesses also contribute immediately to local economic multipliers (see chapter 6) and their owners often fill important community leadership and youth mentorship roles. The scale of working with microbusinesses is also likely to be an easier match for community groups, particularly churches, compared to some other CED strategies. Indeed, for many communities, microbusinesses will be their first foray into CED.

Compared to traditional entrepreneurial endeavors, microbusinesses, also called microenterprises, have relatively few barriers to entry, with minimal capital, educational, and language requirements.[3] Microbusinesses are a popular pathway taken by immigrants who traditionally have played an outsized role in entrepreneurship in the United States, comprising 18 percent of small business owners while representing 14 percent of our population. In fact, one study of street vendors in New York found that 51 percent were immigrants![4]

Notwithstanding their popularity, a myriad of barriers and challenges exist for microbusinesses. Benefits such as sick pay or paid vacation are nearly nonexistent in microbusinesses and working hours can be brutal. The previously cited study on street vendors found that amongst those working full time on their microbusiness, the average working day was eleven hours, five-and-a-half days a week. Needless to say, all small business owners, especially those running microbusinesses, are stretched thin by wearing multiple hats. They have minimal time available for training and outside support, even when desperately needed. The stress of running a business is also a constant, with razor-thin margins and limited savings making financial stress particularly acute. Perhaps the biggest challenge is that microbusiness owners, particularly brand new entrepreneurs, don't know what they don't know. Research from the Association for Enterprise Opportunity (AEO) found a 30 percent increase in revenue growth for businesses that received support, further estimating that "with the right mix of resources and support systems, employment from microbusinesses in low-wealth communities alone could grow by well over 10 percent."[5] Mercy Corps' MicroMentor program has found that mentored entrepreneurs create twice as many jobs as those who work on their own.[6]

---

3. This chapter focuses on "microentrepreneurs" in microbusinesses. See chapter 5 of this book for a discussion of larger scale entrepreneurial activities.

4. Carpenter, *Upwardly Mobile*.

5. Association for Enterprise Opportunity, *Reimagining Technical Assistance*.

6. See the MicroMentor website: https://www.micromentor.org/.

The AEO has developed a framework to ensure that microbusinesses receive the right kind of support that will not only help the entrepreneurs and their businesses succeed, but also recognizes the unique challenges of low-income communities. AEO's "trusted guidance"[7] model recognizes that entrepreneurs will have one of three starting points: (1) those looking to start a business, (2) those who want to grow an existing business, and (3) those looking specifically for access to capital. The framework identifies five needs for microentrepreneurs which should guide the development of training and support programs:

1. *Confidence*: role models, mentoring, business planning

2. *Marketing and Sales*: market analysis, lead generation, social media, creative design

3. *Credit Building*: monitoring of credit scores, strategies for credit score improvement

4. *Financial Management*: budgeting, accounting, taxes

5. *Financing*: knowledge and connections to debt and equity financing

Fortunately, a number of proven training and support systems exist which fulfill the trusted guidance model. The process outlined below is predicated on working with one of several organizations who have proven their systems and now offer assistance in replicating their models.

Getting Started

As with all CED strategies, the place to start is to assess your community's environment and determine if microbusinesses are an appropriate strategy to pursue.[8] For example, is there unused space that microbusinesses could fill? These could be vacant storefronts, space in empty parking lots, and unused church space. Are there clusters of food carts, farmer's markets, pop-up retail, and similar market spaces available for microbusinesses to rent at affordable rates? Who will microbusinesses have to compete with? If your community has easy access to strip malls and big box retailers, would community members welcome local alternatives? Survey your community to estimate how many microbusinesses are already established and if there

7. Association for Enterprise Opportunity, *Reimagining Technical Assistance*.
8. See chapter 13 for a complete CED assessment process.

is an untapped supply of microentrepreneurs looking for the opportunity to start a microbusiness. Look at the demographics of your community and speak with specific immigrant or minority groups to determine their interest in developing businesses. You should also assess your community's training and support environment for microentrepreneurs. Are there any community groups already offering support in areas such as business plan development, financing, or other aspects of starting a business? Given that these are likely piecemeal offerings from a variety of organizations, how do they deliver against the trusted guidance model outlined above? Are the trainings reaching low-income and other marginalized groups effectively?

Second, develop allies into a core team. Include existing and potential microentrepreneurs, local banks and community foundations, community development corporations (CDCs) and other community organizations, and churches from your community. Talk to local business owners who may be running successful small- and medium-sized businesses and encourage them to participate. Don't forget your local anchor institutions (see chapter 11) who may be interested in providing funding to build the local microbusiness environment to support their community building objectives. Together, this core team can develop a vision, determine gaps, and agree on an implementation plan.

Temali's CED handbook identifies five activities that are necessary, at some level, for all successful microbusiness programs: (1) attracting microentrepreneurs, (2) providing training, (3) connecting business to space and other resources, (4) lending, and (5) supporting in a variety of ways such as mentoring and relational support, professional services, coaching in business plan development, and networking connections. With your core team, determine how various organizations within the community can collaborate to deliver these elements, or if a single organization will be funded to provide them all.

As mentioned above, a number of organizations are ready to equip communities with their proven microbusiness training and support programs. We strongly recommend this approach versus a piecemeal approach or developing materials from scratch. See below for details on several recommended organizations with which to engage.

The Role of Churches

Churches have much to contribute to a CED microbusiness endeavor. As Temali points out, one of the primary challenges for a microbusiness program is connecting with microentrepreneurs. The networks within churches can reach potential program participants within an environment built on relationship and trust. Flyers and emails are necessary, but personal invitations and encouragement to attend trainings are most effective. In order to maximize the reach, however, groups of churches must be willing to work together, with the goal of reaching the entire community along all demographic characteristics. Having at least one champion within each church will help generate buy-in and maximize the effectiveness of the church-based network outreach. Of course, partnerships with non-church community organizations is also extremely important in order to reach as many potential microentrepreneurs as possible.

Many churches naturally gravitate to programs that involve training and one-on-one relationship building, making microbusinesses a good fit. Churches can provide trainers, coaches, or mentors, and be important delivery partners in microbusiness training programs. However, it is vital that program leadership and training delivery reflect the community as much as possible. While white, more affluent churches may have experienced business professionals among their attendees, their role as trainers or mentors must be balanced with minorities and lower-income community members who also may have substantial business experience to share.

Churches can also provide space for microbusinesses, whether a makerspace (see chapter 4), commercial kitchen access, office space, or even retail space. For example, the Gresham and Rockwood United Methodist Churches in the Portland metropolitan area teamed up to convert the Rockwood UMC space into the Rockwood Center where "Spirituality and the Arts, Education and Opportunity, Culture and Community come together."[9] The Rockwood Center provides space for microbusiness development, hosting several programs for women entrepreneurs to develop microbusinesses.

Finally, churches can generate significant demand for microbusiness products and services by encouraging attendees to patronize these local businesses. Publishing a directory, highlighting recent training program graduates, and inviting microbusinesses on-site periodically can raise

---

9. See https://www.therockwoodcenter.com/.

awareness for these businesses and their courageous entrepreneurs, driving revenues and increasing the amount of spending that stays within the community.

Challenges

In addition to the primary challenge of reaching microentrepreneurs, actually delivering training and support in such a way that it meets microentrepreneurs where they are at is a significant challenge. Because of time constraints and limited experience in formal educational settings, a variety of training formats should be offered including traditional weekly classes, special workshops, and one-on-one mentoring and coaching. Getting the right mix of trainers who have both business professionalism and community-credible experience is a difficult but important consideration. For example, while bringing in a CEO from a mid-sized business may provide valuable insight into senior-level decision making, it will have limited impact on the realities of a microbusiness owner with no plans to hire even a single employee.

In addition to selecting the right types of training and trainers, programs can struggle if they don't vet potential microentrepreneurs adequately. Temali encourages programs to realistically assess trainees based on their business idea, a strong likelihood that the business will succeed in their community, and willingness to commit time to training. In some cases, the microentrepreneurs are not really interested in learning or changing behaviors but hoping to get access to capital, space, or some other need. A frank discussion of their goals and how the training will or will not help them can save time and frustration for everybody involved.

Case Study: Sunshine Enterprises

Sunshine Enterprises[10] is the small business development arm of a century-old faith-based organization in Chicago called Sunshine Gospel Ministries.[11] Sunshine Enterprises was the first organization to take part in a pilot program to replicate the proven microbusiness curriculum of Rising Tide

10. https://www.sunshineenterprises.com/.
11. https://www.sunshinegospel.org/.

Capital.[12] From its home in Jersey City, New Jersey, Rising Tide Capital has trained over a thousand microentrepreneurs since 2004. After adopting the program in 2013, Sunshine Enterprises has developed three of an envisioned five hubs to bring its program to under-resourced neighborhoods across Chicago. Program offerings include a twelve-week intensive Community Business Academy, business acceleration services, and connections to marketplace and financial capital. Industry-specific cohorts such as construction trades and arts and makers ensure that the training speaks as directly to the entrepreneurs as possible. In addition to their relationship with Rising Tide Capital, the success of the program is predicated on an extensive coalition of partners and supporters, including several community development corporations, financial institutions and foundations, and local governments.

Further Reading and Exploration

Association for Enterprise Opportunity (AEO)

AEO[13] is a wide-ranging association of organizations serving the microbusiness industry. Their innovation-hub model, conferences, and research are important sources of information and support for those looking to establish a microbusiness program in their community.

Mercy Corps MicroMentor Program

An international program that also works with entrepreneurs in the United States, MicroMentor[14] is a proven program that connects entrepreneurs with mentors in an online platform. They offer a partnership program to help local communities integrate MicroMentor into their CED programs.

12. https://partnerships.risingtidecapital.org/.
13. https://aeoworks.org/.
14. https://www.micromentor.org/.

Rising Tide Capital

As highlighted in the case study above, Rising Tide Capital[15] offers their proven training and support program to communities across the country.

Workshop in Business Opportunities (WIBO)

WIBO[16] has been offering training and support to entrepreneurs in under-resourced communities for over fifty years. Their affiliate program enables communities to leverage WIBO's decades of experience to bring proven training and support offerings to local communities.

State and Regional Microenterprise Organizations

There are numerous associations and networks across the country that provide state or region-specific support to microentrepreneurs and local microbusiness training providers. Examples include the California Association for Microenterprise Opportunity (CAMEO),[17] Micro Enterprise Services of Oregon (MESO),[18] and IowaMicroLoan.[19]

---

15. https://partnerships.risingtidecapital.org/.

16. https://wibo.works/.

17. https://cameonetwork.org/.

18. https://www.mesopdx.org/.

19. https://www.iowamicroloan.org/.

4

Makerspaces and the Maker Movement

Overview

THE MAKER MOVEMENT REVOLVES around small-scale, local production of goods, typically by self-employed craftspeople, artisans, or "makers." On a slightly larger scale, the movement includes small businesses that produce and sell small-batch, place-based products that have local flair and flavor.[6] As a CED strategy, the maker movement is a potential source of locally rooted jobs and businesses, leveraging locally sourced supplies and labor to further enhance the local economy through what economists call a multiplier effect. "Makerspaces" are a physical manifestation of the way in which the movement creates local connections and seeks to strengthen community fabric through mutual learning, sharing of space and equipment, and ultimately the development of a community identity.

Portland State University professor (retired) Charles Heying describes the products within an "artisan economy" in his book *Brews to Bikes: Portland's Artisan Economy*, with characteristics including: handmade, designed to age, locally distinct, appreciated rather than just consumed, and egalitarian.[2] While most of the characteristics in this list are relatively self-explanatory, here "egalitarian" refers to removing the distinction between

---

6. While some extend the maker movement to the open design movement in large-scale manufacturing, such as GE's FirstBuild, we find this has less to do with community building and artisan products and more to do with speeding up corporate innovation. Therefore, we exclude it from CED consideration.

2. Heying, *Brew to Bikes*.

"the popular" for the masses and "the fine" reserved for the elite. More broadly, the maker movement is egalitarian in the sense of being highly collaborative and distributed, in contrast to the top-down centralized control of most corporations and large-scale developments. Former Apple executive Peter Hirshberg describes the movement as an open ecosystem with individual participants across a wide swath of society, including organizations from private, nonprofit, and government sectors.[3] As will be seen later, nurturing and activating this ecosystem is a critical component of creating an actual maker movement that can in turn impact a community's economic trajectory.

For maximum success, a maker movement strategy should be integrated with several other strategies highlighted in this book. For example, business incubators and entrepreneur support (chapter 5) can be leveraged to help makers turn their skills and passions into a business that generates income and potentially even jobs. Maker movements can be incorporated into a wholistic workforce development strategy (chapter 7), not only for those interested in self-employment and business creation, but to help participants develop skills to start or advance their career working within existing businesses. Also, with the emphasis on small scale and locality, makers within a community often band together into cooperatives, helping fuel other community-owned and operated enterprises (chapter 6).

Getting Started

Because maker movements are rooted in egalitarianism, perhaps more than any other strategy outlined in this book, starting one in your community requires an open, collaborative approach. The first step is to identify existing resources and start cataloging maker-movement participants, ideally in a crowdsourced, online map.[4] For example, are there any makerspaces already in your community or adjacent communities? Who is active or has been active as a maker in your community? In addition to makerspaces, local farmers markets, craft fairs, maker meetups, and "pop-up" stores are good places to connect with makers. What you may find is that while there may be makers in your community, there is often little connection and no sense of a *movement*.

3. Hirshberg et al., *Maker City*.
4. See https://makerspaces.make.co/ for an example.

In larger communities, if funds are available, a more formal survey of your community's maker ecosystem is an excellent next step. This could be in conjunction with a local university or it could be a project that a maker movement steering team takes on as an initial project. Maker City, in conjunction with the Deloitte Center for the Edge Innovation, has created a maker ecosystem model spanning business/manufacturing, scientific/medical, civic, nonprofit, arts, and education sectors, that can provide a useful guide.[5]

Hirshberg and his colleagues point out that it is not enough to simply map or catalog an ecosystem; for a maker movement strategy to actually take off, it must be activated. This requires somebody to play the role of the "activator" to encourage connection, community building, and ultimately the flow of goods and services. Connections between makers can be nurtured by providing resources that makers may need. For example, based on your mapping and surveying, you may have identified that the nearest makerspace is too far away from your community and decide to start one, something that churches may be particularly well equipped to do, as described in the following section. In addition to providing and retrofitting a space, a makerspace may include equipment to share such as 3D printers, sewing machines, a commercial kitchen, or wood/metal working machines. Helping to procure such equipment and offering it for shared use in a common space can be an excellent way to not only help makers launch their businesses, but it can provide space for intangible community building that is so vital to maker movements and communities in general.

Activation could also entail sponsoring events such as a maker faire or festival. Such events not only provide opportunities for local makers to connect with potential customers, they can also develop connections between makers and encourage newcomers to the movement. While periodic events can be successful to help activate a maker movement, a permanent shared space can be even more impactful, providing business incubation services, shared equipment, and a themed destination for customers to buy and enjoy locally produced goods and services year round. See below for an example, the Portland Mercado.

Maker City provides additional steps for launching and growing a maker movement in your community, including:

5. See Hirshberg et al., *Maker City*, for details.

1. Maker roundtables: bring together makers and interested people and organizations from across the entire maker ecosystem. Collaboratively develop a vision for a maker movement in your community, identify resources and barriers, and galvanize commitment.

2. Maker government liaison: if your community's local government or economic development department doesn't already have one, request a liaison to actively participate in the movement.

3. Develop an education and training strategy: work with local school districts, libraries, and museums to develop maker opportunities for school-age children. Explore partnerships with community colleges who may offer vocational training for prospective makers.

4. Integrate with business incubation and entrepreneurship support services to help makers develop viable businesses.

5. Engage with immigrant populations: Community Development Corporations, churches, and other organizations that serve under-resourced neighborhoods can be excellent partners to engage with immigrants who may already have micro- and small-businesses running, but don't necessarily identify as "makers."

The Role of Churches

Churches are uniquely positioned to help launch and sustain a maker movement in a community. The networking capabilities of churches are nearly unparalleled in our society, with large churches or groups of small churches capable of reaching hundreds to thousands of community members on a regular basis. These networks can be leveraged to reach and engage potential makers, skill/craft mentors, as well as business mentors. Church networks can also be vital channels for product promotion, marketing, supply, and distribution. All of these network connections can be even more powerful in communities where churches are deliberately reaching across social and racial divides, helping immigrants, people of color, and low-income residents to actively participate in a community's emerging maker movement.

Churches can also participate by providing space for a makerspace. While these spaces are often found in repurposed industrial space, unused church office space, gyms, or even sanctuaries could be retrofitted to provide space for makers to ply their trades. Capital in the form of loans or grants could be provided to help individual makers with startup expenses, or larger amounts of capital could be raised to retrofit a new makerspace, complete with shared equipment such as 3D printers, power tools, and machine tools.

Finally, churches can teach and preach a robust, holistic theology of work. This can provide maker movements needed fuel by recognizing the inherent dignity of work, with periodic church celebrations of the creative role of makers. Church attendees can be encouraged to support maker businesses and makerspaces in the hopes of not only providing for the economic needs of individuals and the community, but to strengthen the tie between Sunday and Monday. As Professor Heying notes, an artisan economy "integrates the work of hands, head, and heart,"[6] to which we would add spirit or soul with the active participation of churches in their community's maker movement.

Challenges

While a community maker movement can provide locally rooted jobs, strengthen the fabric of the community, and develop its sense of place, there are also dangers to navigate. Because most locally produced, hand-crafted products are more expensive than their mass-produced equivalents, the movement could be in danger of being coopted by the "gentry." For example, it is difficult to envision a low-income family shopping for expensive hand-made clothes or candles that arguably will last longer than the cheap, mass-produced products available at Walmart. Caution must be taken to ensure that local maker movements do not reinforce gentrification forces by appealing solely to white, middle-class individuals looking for a sense of the "authentic."

However, while the consumers of the maker movement may initially be tilted towards middle- and upper-incomes, the makers themselves need not be. It is widely reported that immigrants are more likely to be self-employed than native-born residents. One bulwark against the gentrification of the maker movement is to actively encourage immigrants to get involved in the artisan economy. Often, this could simply mean walking alongside immigrant-owned small businesses that are already running, welcoming them into local business networks and providing support, if needed, in the form of financial and social capital. Similarly, working in low-income

6. Heying, *Brew to Bikes*, 40.

and other marginalized communities to develop maker skills and provide support for business creation are central components of an "un-gentrified" maker movement.

Case Study: Maker's Center

Leveraging a building one of its members was looking to donate, along with funds from the church and a local foundation, the Maker's Center[7] is a new endeavor of the Bible Center Church in Charleston, West Virginia. Their new makerspace will run on a subscription model providing access to a CNC wood-cutting machine, 3D laser printer, and an augmented reality design application. The church explains the Maker's Center as a vehicle to provide greater presence in the city by following Jesus' command to love our neighbors as ourselves, operating as a "billboard for gospel renewal." The focus of the center is on developing skills within their community to help reverse the effects of persistent poverty and lack of opportunity. A partnership with a local elementary school recognizes that developing a "maker mindset" of creative problem solving and critical thinking early is key to future success in our ever-evolving economy. The church has developed partnerships with several nearby recovery centers, enabling residents to earn membership points by attending a variety of church-offered classes. The center provides a place to develop skills as varied as phone etiquette, shop safety, computer skills, cake decorating, 3D printing, construction, woodworking, and even driver's education. This later offering reflects the church's ability to leverage the skills of church members, in this case a retiring driver's education teacher, to expand the center's offerings and connect Sunday to Monday for church members.

Further Reading and Exploration

Brew to Bikes: Portland's Artisan Economy

For those looking for a big picture view of the maker movement, Heying's book[8] positions the "artisan economy" within our post-industrial economy as a protest against passive consumption and mass production. The book is

7. https://www.biblecenterchurch.com/city/makers/.
8. See Heying, Brew to Bikes.

based on research of hundreds of local businesses as varied as bike manufacturers, microbreweries, and traditional crafts. While not a "how to," this intriguing book provides context and vision for how a maker movement can tap into deeply rooted longings for belonging and authenticity, areas that the gospel can certainly speak to and cultivate.

Maker City: A Practical Guide for Reinventing our Cities

An excellent overview and call to action, this online book[9] provides practical steps to launch a maker movement in your community. Its ecosystem model, previously referenced in this chapter, shows how maker movements drive civic engagement and intersect with a variety of arenas including education, workforce development, manufacturing, and real estate. The Maker City project is a very helpful resource providing numerous case studies, showing the importance of community connections for vibrant and sustainable CED.

Makerspace: Towards a New Civic Infrastructure

A well-researched article[10] that provides a needed counter-balance to the boosterism of some maker zealots, raising questions on the sustainability of the maker movement and some challenges communities may face along the way.

Artisan Asylum

Want to see what is possible? This nonprofit[11] in the Boston area provides a full-range of learning, teaching, and making oriented around fabrication.

9. See Hirshberg et al., *Maker City*.

10. See Holman, "Makerspace."

11. See https://artisansasylum.com/.

Portland Mercado

Mentioned previously in this chapter, Portland Mercado[12] is centered on a shared commercial kitchen, providing business advising and permanent space for food-oriented businesses. A good example of the intersection of the maker movement with food, immigrant cultures, and third-spaces for community connection.

12. See https://www.portlandmercado.org/.

5

Business Incubators and Entrepreneurs

Overview

THE "ENTREPRENEUR" HAS TAKEN on almost mythical qualities in America. Visions of Edison or Ford creating products and companies that literally changed the world, or twenty-five-year-old Silicon Valley geniuses driving Ferraris after a big IPO, fill our collective imaginations. Indeed, entrepreneurial activity *is* marked by innovation and incredible motivation: entrepreneurs not only believe there is a way to achieve something new, they also believe it is worth pursuing with utter abandon, often to the detriment of health and relationships. The concept has been redeemed and expanded somewhat with the qualifier "social" to point out that many entrepreneurs are driven by a desire to create positive social change rather than just make money. Further, the myth of the individual entrepreneur achieving greatness on their own has been replaced with the recognition that true success requires significant collaboration. There are therefore two sides to the entrepreneurial coin: the individual entrepreneur on one side, and the environment to support and foster entrepreneurial business activity on the other side. CED provides support directly to underserved entrepreneurs while focusing on environmental strategies such as improving connections with capital; providing support services to help launch new businesses; and efforts to attract suppliers, customers, and labor to support entrepreneurial businesses.

In one sense, any business creation activity is "entrepreneurial" and not reserved for one-in-a-million pioneers such as Edison, Ford, Gates, or Musk. For example, we've already delved into the world of the microentre-preneur and microbusiness in chapter 3, seeing innovation and motivation at work in these millions of very small businesses. At the same time, it is important that we are not overly broad in our use of the term "entrepre-neurial" or our CED strategies will become unfocused and inefficient. To aid in achieving focus, researchers provide a useful distinction between three types of business creation strategies: (1) small business development, what we have referred to as microbusinesses above, (2) new business devel-opment, with a focus on supporting new businesses of all types, and (3) en-trepreneurial business development, focusing on growth-oriented ventures with some form of fundamental innovation at their core.[1]

In many, if not most communities, there are very likely already TED efforts underway to support business creation of types two and three from the list above. CED recognizes that such traditional approaches, however, often exclude marginalized people and communities. In these cases, the role of CED is to open up these programs and opportunities to those who are currently excluded or otherwise underserved. In some cases, CED practitioners may be called upon to start new programs that serve these populations as a central goal and not simply as an afterthought. We advise focusing CED strategies around microbusiness development (type one) and new business incubators (type two). Such a focus provides many op-tions for the types of businesses you can assist while avoiding the "high risk, high reward" of type three entrepreneurial development strategies.[2] For our purposes, we distinguish between type one microbusiness development (al-ready covered in chapter 3) and type two business incubation, based on the business's prospects for growth. Type two business development strategies target businesses with substantially larger growth projections than the type one microbusiness thresholds that typically top out at $100,000 in revenue with up to five employees. More on screening for type two businesses will be discussed below.

"Business incubators" is a catch-all term that encompasses a wide va-riety of business nurturing activities. For example, incubators may support very early stage companies with below market rate office space and help writing a business plan. Or they can provide services for more established

1. Malizia and Feser, *Understanding Local Economic Development*.
2. Malizia and Feser, *Understanding Local Economic Development*.

companies looking to expand through the services of a "business accelerator." Most metropolitan areas will already have a wide variety of business incubation programs such as one-stop business assistance centers offered by local governments, nonprofit small business development centers focused on training and mentoring, industry-specific cohorts and business associations, and groups focused on fostering social enterprises. Co-working spaces run by nonprofits and for-profit companies could also be considered a form of business incubation by providing space and fostering community between entrepreneurs. Some incubators focus on helping companies land angel and venture capital investment through networking, business coaching, and help with investor pitches. Needless to say, the range of services and options is dizzying!

Getting Started

It is critical to perform a thorough assessment of the services in and around your community before considering offering any business incubation services.[3] Equally important is to determine if these services are reaching your community and the constituency you desire to serve. Unfortunately, in many cases the answer will be no. However, before jumping in to either replicate these services or to build bridges between these services and your community, it is wise to query your community to determine which services are most needed. In some cases, the most valuable role you can play may be to expose your community to the universe of business incubation services already available and help prepare entrepreneurs and future entrepreneurs for such services. Your community assessment should include specifics on the types of help entrepreneurs need, as well as the types of businesses they have formed or desire to form. This can help to focus the efforts of your business incubator by identifying a niche that is not currently being met by existing services.

Many view business incubation services too simplistically by assuming that providing space and community will somehow result in successful, employment-producing business ventures. In reality, starting a full-fledged business incubator is a formidable task, on par or perhaps more complex than starting a business venture.[4] A distilled list of key elements found in many successful business incubators includes:

3. See chapter 13 for our CED assessment framework.

4. For example, see Ryzhonkov, "Business Incubation Models," for an overview of over twenty different business incubator models.

1. Space and basic business support services

2. Mentors and training

3. Access to specialized equipment

4. Credibility and screening

Items 1 through 3 will be included in the discussion below on the role of churches in business incubation. The fourth item, credibility, is an often overlooked requirement that can be achieved by developing a strong support network of business professionals and successful entrepreneurs, as well as partnering with nonprofits, universities, and local governments who also provide business support services. Anchor institutions (chapter 11) can often be tapped to provide not only credibility but startup funding for business incubators, especially when the focus of the business incubator is to support the building of a localized procurement strategy (chapter 6). It is particularly important for churches to pursue such credibility-building partnerships, because, on their own, most churches will not be able to generate the needed business credibility.

Credibility is an important aspect of business incubation because it will not only convince busy entrepreneurs that your organization can provide them real value, it will also reflect on the graduates of your program, making it easier for them to get funding and additional support in the future. A business incubator's credibility is often reflected in how it determines which businesses to support and in a sense put their stamp of approval on as they complete the program. However, here we must be careful not to reinforce practices of TED that tend to favor white, middle- and upper-class entrepreneurs that are already well connected. To achieve CED objectives, business incubators must exercise prudent business judgment in screening applicants while providing opportunities for traditionally underserved people and communities. Having successful entrepreneurs and businesspeople on your advisory board is crucial to ensure that your business incubator screens for businesses that have the potential for growth and employment that can in turn benefit the entire community. The Real-Win-Worth framework[5] can be useful to develop a set of screening criteria, asking questions such as "Is the market and the product real?"; "Can the company be competitive?"; and "Is there potential for substantial profits and sales?" While there may be the temptation to open your business

5. For detials, see Day, "Is It Real? Can We Win? Is It Worth Doing?"

incubator to whomever in your community is willing to come, keep in mind that the market and customers will not be so welcoming. Better to ask the hard questions during a stringent screening process than to enable a business that is destined to fail.

The Role of Churches

Churches can be vital partners in starting or expanding business incubation services that reach their underserved communities. From items one through three in the list above, a number of key business incubation elements can be provided by churches that directly support an existing business incubator or fit into a broader business incubator system.

Space and Basic Business Support Services

Churches can make office space or warehouse space available to new business ventures in their community. Depending on the church's financial situation, this space can be provided at market rates to support their own financial viability, or below market rates, particularly in support of goals such as nurturing women- or minority-owned businesses. Additional business services may be provided such as reception, access to business equipment (printers, computers, phones, office supplies), conference rooms, janitorial services, and accounting/bookkeeping.

Mentors and Training

A key element of business incubation is connection to experienced entrepreneurs. Church members can be recruited as volunteer mentors to provide industry-specific expertise as well as help in developing a business plan. In some cases, more formal training programs are offered that take a cohort of entrepreneurs through a complete curriculum.[6] Churches can sponsor such training by providing space, curriculum licensing fees, and stipends for trainers.

---

6. See Further Reading and Exploration below for several examples.

Access to Specialized Equipment

Churches can provide access to equipment such as commercial kitchens or wood/metal working tools to help new businesses get off the ground. See chapter 4 for more details on makerspace support.

Challenges

Although entrepreneurship among minorities and women is growing quite rapidly, tremendous racial disparities continue in terms of business creation rates and ability to secure investment funds.[7] CED, particularly church-based CED, must advocate to connect underrepresented and underserved entrepreneurs to business incubation services to ensure that existing lines of inequality are not perpetuated. While prudent screening criteria such as that discussed above must be utilized, the reality is that many of the entrepreneurs and businesses that need the most help are not yet at the stage where they are ready to participate in a business incubator. Thus, what may be needed are "pre-business incubation" classes and services to help these entrepreneurs develop their concepts and businesses to a stage where they can successfully pass the selection criteria to enter a business incubator.

Another challenge is that while traditional business incubators may measure success based solely on the outcomes of the businesses with which they work, CED seeks to tie business creation and business success to overall community thriving. Achieving this, particularly in under resourced communities is challenging, requiring integration with several other CED and community development strategies. For maximum impact, the businesses nurtured via business incubation should hire employees from the community (see chapter 7 on workforce development), be located in spaces/buildings in the community, participate in localized procurement networks (chapter 11), and be active members of community-rooted economies (chapter 6).

7. See "Data Shows Black Entrepreneurship Growing Across the United States."

Case Studies

The Mix

The Mix[8] is a co-working space that helps incubate nonprofit and culinary businesses. Located in repurposed space in the White Rock United Methodist Church in East Dallas, The Mix provides office co-working space, a commercial kitchen, and opportunity to interact with experienced culinary professionals. The Mix is representative of a very popular type of church-based business incubation service focused on providing space and connections. Although on the lower end of the spectrum of potential services, its impact is notably strengthened by focusing its efforts on a specific industry segment, in this case, culinary businesses.

OCEAN

On the other end of the spectrum is OCEAN,[9] a full-spectrum business incubator and accelerator associated with the Crossroads megachurch in Cincinnati, Ohio. Started by Procter & Gamble employees, the church literally has entrepreneurship and business built into its genes, along with the credibility that comes from the active support of experienced Procter & Gamble employees and alumni. OCEAN provides an intense business incubator program, a sixteen-week business accelerator program, connections to mentors and investors, as well as the opportunity to procure seed funding from Ocean Capital. While OCEAN infuses its training with faith, it accepts participants of all faiths or no faith.

Hustle PHX

Hustle PHX[10] is a faith-based nonprofit in South Phoenix that focuses on nurturing entrepreneurship amongst those typically outside of the formal economy. Hustle PHX provides online learning sponsored by the Acton School of Business, connections with mentors, and the opportunity to pitch for funding. Strong partnerships with churches provide space for classes in convenient locations, as well as opportunities for church members to

8. See https://themixcoworking.com/.

9. See https://oceanprograms.com/.

10. See https://hustlephx.com/.

provide vital coaching and mentoring in their areas of expertise such as law, finance, marketing, HR, and more.

Further Reading and Exploration

Harlem Commonwealth Council

Although not faith-based, Harlem Commonwealth Council[11] is an excellent example of a full-spectrum business incubation service that is integrated with related services such as youth and adult education as well as real estate investment/development.

Center for Faith and Work

The Redeemer Presbyterian Church of New York's Center for Faith and Work[12] encourages and supports entrepreneurs within the congregation to build businesses that change lives, provide humanizing work, and engage with brokenness. Training and support to develop you own Center is available.

INTERiSE

INTERiSE[13] is a national organization that provides research and training to support small businesses at all stages of growth. Their "Streetwise" MBA program is available for licensing, enabling new business incubators to provide a proven training curriculum to their community of entrepreneurs.

Make Good Social Entrepreneurship Accelerator Course

The Social Entrepreneurship Accelerator Course[14] from Make Good is a three-part social entrepreneurship course that incorporates peer learning and a final "Pitch & Pledge" culminating event into a fast-paced, intensive

11. See https://www.harlemcommonwealth.org/.
12. See https://faithandwork.com/programs/7-entrepreneurship-innovation.
13. See https://interise.org/.
14. See https://rootedgood.org/make-good/.

experience. The founding organization, Rooted Good, offers training and licensing for those interested in bringing the course to their community.

Ryzhonkov, "Business Incubation Models"

An overview[15] of over twenty different business incubation models used throughout the world.

Athey, "Thinking about setting up a new business incubator or accelerator?"

A useful article[16] with definitions and an overview of business incubators and accelerators. Provides key success factors and best practices in establishing new incubators and accelerators.

Day, "Is It Real? Can We Win? Is It Worth Doing?"

A freely available Harvard Business Review article[17] that provides a useful overview of the Real-Win-Worth framework that can form the basis of a business incubator's screening process.

---

15. See Ryzhonkov, "Business Incubation Models."
16. See Athey, "Thinking about setting up a new business incubator or accelerator?"
17. See Day, "Is It Real? Can We Win? Is It Worth Doing?"

6

Cooperatives and Community-Rooted Economics

Overview

THE CONCEPT OF COMMUNITY-ROOTED economics is best captured with the mantra "people over capital." A CED strategy centered on developing locally rooted business drives more overall community wealth than a strategy chasing highly mobile and fickle big business. The experience of many communities over the last four decades highlights the allure and danger of this latter, TED approach. Communities across the country have experienced frenetic business expansions with good jobs followed by the shuttering of those same businesses as they flee overseas in search of cheaper labor. We've also seen distant investors destroy locally grown businesses by selling off the assets to the highest bidder. Many communities have made way for big-box retailers offering low prices on a mindboggling array of products from all over the world, even as local retailers and suppliers are forced out of business. And of course, there is the as-yet evolving impact of the ubiquitous Amazon Prime delivery truck. During this time, we've experienced a massive transition of work from relatively stable, living-wage jobs with benefits to low-wage service jobs with minimal benefits. CED recognizes that economic growth that generates profits for distant shareholders and investors is benefiting only a small portion of society, with low-income and other marginalized populations being left out of the bounty. A commitment to community-rooted economics, also called by various other terms such as "economic democracy"[1] and "solidarity economies,"[2] provides communities not only broad-based opportunity but resilience in the face of ever-changing global business environments.

Key to community-rooted economics is local ownership of assets that can take many forms, including locally owned for-profit businesses, larger businesses that provide employee stock ownership plans (ESOPs), worker cooperatives, and municipal enterprises such as local utilities. Anchor institutions can be considered members of a community-rooted economy, particularly when they follow localized procurement strategies (chapter 11). Community-rooted economies also create a broader vision for what is considered "economic," embracing a diverse view that includes sharing systems, informal economies, time banks, and local currencies.

The central economic principle that turns a community-rooted economy into an equitable wealth generator is the "economic multiplier" effect. Analysts determine economic multipliers based on how much of each dollar spent with a particular business is circulated back into the community versus being deposited into the bank accounts of companies and investors outside of the community. For example, a portion of each dollar you spend at a local business is used by that business to pay employees who in turn spend money in the community, as well as purchasing goods and services needed to run their business. If these goods and services are procured from other local businesses, the money continues to circulate within the community. That same dollar spent at a big box retailer will still have a portion going towards local workers' wages, but the vast majority will immediately evaporate from the community to pay global suppliers, headquarters personnel, and distant investors. The difference in multipliers can be substantial: research has shown that $100 spent at a local food cooperative generates $164 for the local economy, compared to $137 when spent at a conventional grocer, a difference of over 20 percent.[3]

As discussed in chapter 11, localized procurement strategies by large anchor organizations can keep a tremendous amount of capital in a community. This same concept applies to businesses of all sizes and forms that are willing to make a commitment to local procurement. The economic multiplier effect is potentially even stronger when coupled with cooperative

1. Casper-Futterman and Defilippis, *On Economic Democracy.*

2. Loh and Shear, *Solidarity Economy.*

3. Kelly et al., *Broad-Based Ownership Models,* 17.

businesses that distribute wealth more broadly than traditional business ventures, particularly towards marginalized populations that are underrepresented as owners and investors in privately owned businesses. Because this topic is large enough for a separate book-length treatment, our discussion will focus on increasing this economic multiplier effect in an equitable manner with worker cooperatives and the development of mutually supporting, local business networks to keep capital within the community.

Although the precursors to modern worker cooperatives, such as those associated with European craft guilds and monastic orders, have been in existence for literally millennia, most Americans are only familiar with consumer or retail cooperatives established for the purposes of consumption. According to the United States Federation of Worker Cooperatives,[4] there were approximately 465 worker cooperatives in the United States as of 2018. A recent Democracy at Work report provides an excellent definition of a worker cooperative:

> Worker cooperatives are values-driven businesses that put worker and community benefit at the core of their purpose. The members of the cooperative are the people who work in it. These typically small and medium-sized businesses can be found in every sector and industry, from engineering and manufacturing to retail to service. Workers participate in the profits, oversight, and, to varying degrees, the management of the organization, using democratic practices. Workers own the majority of the equity in the business and control the voting shares.[5]

Getting Started

Establishing a community-rooted economy is a long-term endeavor, requiring an ecosystem to nurture the development and growth of locally rooted businesses along with efforts to strengthen the connections between those businesses. We recommend a parallel-path approach: (1) develop a mutually supporting business network focused on localized procurement and equitable economic growth, and (2) build the ecosystem from which to grow and establish worker cooperatives.

4. https://www.usworker.coop.
5. Hoover and Abell, *Cooperative Growth Ecosystem*, 3.

Mutually Supporting Business Networks

The best place to start building mutually supporting business networks is with existing, locally rooted businesses. Business incubation and entrepreneur support (chapter 5), makerspaces (chapter 4), and micro-business support (chapter 3) can complement this strategy by nurturing and strengthening locally grown businesses. Most communities have a Chamber of Commerce where you can make inquiries if there are already efforts underway to support the community through localized procurement strategies. If you or members of your faith community have already started businesses, consider joining your local Chamber of Commerce, as well as a business networking group such as LeTip.[6] Such groups exist to exchange qualified leads and are an excellent place to start solidifying relationships between local businesses and identify opportunities to localize procurement. There are also a wide variety of "Christian" business networking groups that should be explored, but as described in chapter 1, you should not assume that these marketplace ministry organizations are necessarily aligned with the central tenants of CED. Our country has also seen a movement towards "values-driven" businesses in the form of B Corps, employee-owned businesses, social enterprises, and various types of cooperatives. Identifying and connecting with businesses from these varied sources is likely to uncover allies with which to form your core team. Finally, anchor institutions such as hospitals, universities, or museums can provide a significant demand for local goods and services and be the impetus for localized procurement strategies to emerge. See chapter 11 for more information on how to start working with local anchors.

Regardless of how you connect with existing local business networks, it is important to create a shared vision for the equitable wealth building that localized procurement strategies can provide. Sharing examples (see below) can help to build such a shared vision, as well as working together through books and educational materials on CED, cooperatives, and equitable economies. The goal is to build a core group of business leaders committed not only to the business benefits of localized procurement, but to the larger goals of CED. Throughout the process, pilot projects should be identified to develop procurement relationships amongst core team members and their business networks.

---

6. https://letip.com. Hundreds of local chapters exist throughout the United States.

A more formal mechanism to support localized procurement can be achieved through the development of a platform to connect local businesses, area anchor institutions, and nonprofits, with each other. BronXchange,[7] a project of the Bronx Cooperative Development Initiative, seeks to keep the billions spent on goods and services by area institutions from bypassing local businesses. The organization vets Bronx-based vendors, connects them with institutional purchasers, and provides business services and support to streamline the transactions. The BronXchange exists within a larger effort to promote economic democracy including workforce development, business incubation, and leadership development.

Local currencies provide another mechanism to instill foundations for local purchasing and procurement. While somewhat novel in our day, local currencies were much more common in the early 1900s. See below for links to more information.

Developing a Cooperative Growth Ecosystem

The Democracy at Work Institute and Project Equity have developed a framework for communities interested in developing worker cooperatives. As seen in Table 1, the Cooperative Growth Ecosystem (CGE) identifies four essential building blocks, four accelerators, and three environmental elements that comprise a complete ecosystem. Interested readers should reference the framework document for complete details.[8]

---

7. https://bronxchange.com.
8. See Hoover and Abell, *Cooperative Growth Ecosystem*.

TABLE 1: ELEMENTS OF COOPERATIVE GROWTH ECOSYSTEM[9]

Essential Elements	Skills & Capacity	Business and management skills; entrepreneurial and business growth experience
	Financing	Connections and experience to access loan capital, investment capital, grants
	Technical Assistance	Legal, accounting, human resources, and related professional services
	Cooperative Developers	Cooperative growth expertise, training, advising
Growth Accelerators	Business Support	Incubators, peer networks, workforce development
	Connection to Market	Anchor institutions, community benefits agreements, business networks
	Policy	Laws, regulations to support cooperative development; tax incentives
	Advocacy Partnerships	Connections to social movements, faith communities, government official support
Legitimization	Values-driven Businesses	Network of cooperatives, B Corps, social enterprises
	Attitudes and Culture	General ethos of inclusive economic growth; pro-cooperative attitudes
	Cooperative Education	Incorporation of cooperatives into business schools, college, secondary education, entrepreneur training, business incubators

Develop Your Coalition

Building on your core team of business leaders discussed above, the elements in Table 1 identify where else to identify members for a guiding coalition who will establish the community vision, analyze the existing ecosystem, and shepherd the process forward. In addition to foundations, bankers, accountants, and lawyers who will provide essential services, you should reach out to government officials, community organizations, other faith communities, and nonprofits involved in economic justice and economic development to join your coalition. A key element of the CGE framework, cooperative developers, highlights the importance of connecting to existing worker cooperatives or dedicated nonprofits who provide advisory and consultative services for those interested in starting their own worker cooperative. Examples of cooperative developers are provided below.

9. Adapted from Hoover and Abell, *Cooperative Growth Ecosystem*, 8.

Follow a Context-Specific, Flexible Process

While the CGE describes a generic process, its power is its ability to in-corporate a diversity of contexts for cooperative development. In regions such as New York or San Francisco, a robust entrepreneurial and coop-erative ecosystem already exists, so the challenge is to bring the benefits of such an ecosystem into forgotten corners of the city. In most communities, however, many years of work will be necessary to develop such a mature ecosystem. While this should remain as a long-term goal, short-term wins should also be pursued to build momentum and garner additional support for the movement. A number of starting points and potential paths exist, all dependent on your specific context. Examples include:

- Your community may have a socially minded, entrepreneurial en-vironment with experienced business creators and leaders who are interested in immediately jumping in to create a new worker coopera-tive. While they may not have explicit experience with cooperatives, connecting them to a cooperative development organization can guide their business acumen towards the development of a sustainable worker cooperative.

- In other cases, the ideal starting point is to identify an existing business that may be a candidate for conversion to a worker cooperative. This can include business owners nearing retirement, such as Bob Moore of Bob's Red Mill Natural Foods who turned the entire company over to employees through an ESOP.[10] South Mountain Company, an archi-tecture and building firm located in Martha's Vineyard, was founded in 1975 and converted to a worker cooperative in 1986. See below for a University of Wisconsin report on more cooperative transitions with several case studies.

- Anchor institutions can play critical roles in developing community-rooted economies, including providing funding to start new coopera-tives. Evergreen Cooperative, perhaps the most well-known worker cooperative in the United States, was launched with a $1 million grant by University Hospitals in Cleveland, OH. See chapter 11 for more details.

- If your work in developing a mutually supporting business network is going well, as witnessed by a number of successful localized pro-curement relationships, build on this momentum to start a worker

10. Tims, "Founder of Bob's Red Mill Natural Foods transfers business to employees."

cooperative to fill any unmet market needs in the procurement network. With a localized procurement network in place, even in nascent form, it will be easier to gain financing support to develop a worker cooperative if you can point to a local market ready for the goods or services to be delivered by the new cooperative.

The Role of Churches

The Mondragon cooperative system was founded by a Catholic priest, Jose Maria Arizmendiarrieta, combining his religious foundations rich in Catholic social teaching with concern for the high rates of unemployment in his region of Basque country. Closer to home, the Intercommunity Justice and Peace Center, a collective of various faith communities in the Cincinnati area, was instrumental in starting Co-op Cincy, a cooperative developer founded in 2009. While churches and the faith community can certainly play central, even pivotal roles in community-rooted economies and cooperative development, more likely are roles that emphasize support and network development.

Congregations can support cooperatives of various types through their purchasing activities and in the process learn more about cooperatives. For example, Equal Exchange is a worker cooperative providing fair-trade coffee and related items nationwide, with a program designed specifically for coffee-hungry congregations. Participating in cooperatives, even as a consumer, can help churches build awareness for cooperatives amongst members and leaders, potentially opening the door for more active involvement in supporting the creation of worker cooperatives in their communities.

While some church pastors may be seasoned business owners and business leaders, many churches' pews are filled with them. Church members who own or run businesses can be valuable allies in developing the business networks to support localized procurement programs.[11] Church members with legal and financial expertise may also be able to fill important ecosystem roles to support the development of worker cooperatives. Finally, learning about worker cooperatives and the power of localized procurement strategies, perhaps accompanied by field trips to cities with successful programs in place, can help solidify support from church members and cement the ties between Sunday and Monday.

11. Partnerships with more affluent suburban churches should also be considered to build business networks for localized procurement programs.

Challenges

While economic theorists may debate how local economies start and grow, it is quite uncontroversial that the long-term economic viability of a region requires some "export base"[12] that brings a steady flow of capital into the local economy. The importance of an export base is seen in areas where the predominant industry has evaporated, such as logging towns, with very little left on which to build economic activity. While many cites have over-emphasized the export base through TED strategies to attract large companies, the strategies outlined in this chapter will struggle to gain a foothold if a metropolitan area's export base is declining significantly. In these cases, a new export base must be established to bring capital back into the community, a topic beyond the scope of this book.

Another challenge is that worker cooperatives face the same economic and market realities as other forms of business. Simply converting a declining factory to a worker cooperative will likely fail if the market for that factory's goods is evaporating because of fundamental market shifts. Thus, traditional market-analysis and strategic-planning skills are required to ensure that the goods and services provided will fill a market need and that the worker cooperative will be successful against competitors.

Finally, establishing a community-rooted economy is a long-term strategy. Maintaining commitment over a ten-to-fifteen-year timeframe, perhaps even longer, requires consistency in guiding leadership. A challenge for the strategies outlined above is to find an organizational home to provide this consistency and establish alignment with other long-term initiatives such as community development.

Case Studies

Daily Bread Cooperative

Daily Bread[13] was founded in 1980 as a worker cooperative in England, continuing to this day as a thriving business with a strong Christian ethos.[14] Founder Roger Sawtell was motivated to start a business venture that

12. Economists consider an industry to be part of the "export base," or basic economy, if the primary sales are to customers outside of the region. This is contrasted with localized, non-basic businesses such as retail and services that serve a region's residents.

13. https://www.dailybread.co.uk/.

14. See Voinea, "How has religious faith—or the lack of it—driven co-operative culture?"

reflected Christian principles, drawing on his Quaker background with consensual decision making and landing on the worker cooperative model. At its founding, Daily Bread drew on members of the St. Peters Church who were convinced that concern for people over profits could generate substantial common good and a successful business. What is perhaps most notable about Daily Bread is its longevity and embeddedness in the community, with strong ties to the town of Northhampton and support of local initiatives to address poverty and the causes of homelessness.

Community Purchasing Alliance

Community Purchasing Alliance is a purchasing cooperative that provides Washington DC-area churches and other mission-driven organizations access to services such as HVAC, electricity and natural gas utilities, landscaping, trash hauling, and more. Cooperative members save substantially through group purchasing, and in the process support local businesses with 58 percent of 2019 contracts awarded to small, local businesses.[15]

Further Reading and Exploration
Cooperative Growth Ecosystem

This free report[16] by the Democracy at Work Institute and Project Equity, referred to above, provides an extensive overview of developing a cooperative ecosystem, including a number of case studies.

Community-Wealth Worker Cooperative Overview

An online treasure trove of information including best practices, case studies, and a link to support organizations.[17]

---

15. See https://www.cpa.coop/.
16. Hoover and Abell, *Cooperative Growth Ecosystem.*
17. See "Overview: Worker Cooperatives."

OpLaw

Legal information and best practices to support cooperatives, including a state-by-state guide.[18]

Cooperative Entrepreneurship Curriculum

Open-source educational materials to explore the development of a cooperative.[19]

United States Federation of Worker Cooperatives— Technical Assistance Services

From the leading worker-cooperative organization, a substantial collection of training materials and information on accessing technical assistance.[20]

University of Wisconsin Report on Cooperative Conversions

A variety of case studies on the conversion of privately held businesses to worker cooperatives.[21]

Cooperation for Liberation

An informal study and working group focused on cooperative economic development strategies in Black communities.[22]

Center for Community-Based Enterprise (C2BE)

C2BE[23] is a cooperative incubator for Black-owned and worker-owned businesses in Detroit. C2BE provides consulting and support for entrepreneurs as well as established business enterprises interested in converting to a worker-cooperative model. Their work includes building a local ecosystem to

18. www.co-oplaw.org.

19. See http://northcountryfoundation.org/collectingourselves.

20. See https://www.usworker.coop/coopclinic/.

21. See Berner et al., *Successful Cooperative Ownership Transitions*.

22. See https://kola.groups.io/g/coop4lib.

23. See https://c2be.org/.

support neighborhood-based ventures, including a partnership with Detroit Community Wealth Fund to provide "non-extractive" startup loans.

Bronx Cooperative Development Initiative

A community-led organization on the forefront of establishing community-rooted economies. Developers of the BronXchange platform described above, they also provide training resources including an "Economic Democracy Learning Center."[24]

Co-op Cincy

A cooperative developer providing valuable materials, including a "Co-op U."[25]

Rice, *Buy Newark: A Guide to Promoting Economic Inclusion through Local Purchasing*

An excellent report on the benefits of local procurement strategies with guidance and case studies.[26]

Schumacher Center Local Currencies Program

Extensive information on local currencies and how they can be used to support local businesses and increase local economic multipliers.[27]

Berkshares Local Currency Program

An example of a successful local currency program with the support of local banks and over four-hundred locally owned businesses.[28]

24. See https://bcdi.nyc/.
25. See https://coopcincy.org/.
26. Rice, *Buy Newark*.
27. See https://centerforneweconomics.org/.
28. See http://www.berkshares.org/.

7

Workforce Development

Overview

OUR NATION'S WORKFORCE DEVELOPMENT system comprises a large, complex collection of federal, state, and local government agencies; public and private educational institutions; employers; and nonprofits.[1] Large amounts of government funds are spent in support of this system because of the central role that a well-equipped workforce has in a functioning economy. However, this funding has declined over time, creating constraints on a system that is simultaneously seeing increased demand. In addition, increasing disparities in wage and employment prospects persist, highlighting the tremendous need and opportunity for CED to bring the benefits of workforce development to underserved, marginalized people and communities. As a CED strategy, workforce development taps into the tremendous potential of having all community members employed to a level of self-sufficiency,[2] bringing more dollars into the local economy and contributing to the thriving of all.

While definitions vary, "Human Resource Development" is an umbrella term for the entire range of education and training to support employment, including foundational training such as high-school completion,

1. For an excellent overview of the workforce-development system, see Eyster et al., *Understanding Local Workforce Systems*.

2. See http://www.selfsufficiencystandard.org/ for the definition and calculation of a self-sufficient income for your area.

college preparation, and college graduation support. It is well documented that lifetime wages go up dramatically with education levels, but because of the long timeframes and indirect impact on local economies, such offerings are typically incorporated into broader community-development programs rather than CED programs. "Workforce Development," on the other hand, has more direct and near-term implications for CED goals, with a focus on preparing and connecting people to jobs. Within workforce development, a variety of focus areas exist including (1) aiding new workforce entrants such as high school students, new college graduates, new immigrants, and those on welfare; (2) helping to place laid-off/displaced workers into new careers; and (3) helping low-wage earners move into living wage/good jobs (chapter 9).

CED-based workforce-development efforts, driven by a desire to bring economic thriving to entire communities, typically look for a niche that is currently not being served successfully by the larger workforce-development apparatus. This could be the hard-to-hire such as ex-offenders, those struggling with addiction, immigrants with Limited English Proficiency (LEP), minorities who are shunted into low-wage jobs, and other community members who may be unable to find or keep employment that can lead to self-sufficiency.

There are a variety of services that workforce-development programs may offer. These exist along a continuum from preparation to support after placement:

1. *Preparation*: this type of "soft skills" training prepares participants for success in the job market in areas such as phone/email etiquette, interviewing, conflict resolution at work, dress/clothing, time management, and effective work habits. Also includes strengths/skills assessment and career coaching.

2. *Training*: "hard skills" training develops specific competencies required for a job, often industry- or domain-specific. Such training can be used to help displaced workers retool for a new industry, or to provide low-wage earners more opportunities for advancement.

3. *Placement*: connecting program participants with specific employment opportunities.

4. *Retention support*: keeping a job may require help in areas such as reliable transportation, affordable childcare, financial coaching, legal

advocacy, and more. Also includes providing guidance in mapping out next steps for advancement and achieving self-sufficiency.

Successful workforce development not only works with potential employees, but it also pays attention to the demand for jobs, working with local employers to understand their employment needs and career ladders. And while CED-based workforce development is focused on specific community assets and needs, it also takes into account larger regional economic development trends such as growing (or declining) industry clusters, major new employers, and anticipated corporate expansion (or downsizing) plans.

Getting Started

Because the landscape for workforce development is so complex, a critical first step it to get educated on the system as a whole, understanding the variety of players, how they fit together, and what funding may be available. Such an effort will also help you understand potential gaps that your CED program can fill, and how your efforts fit into the larger workforce-development system. Because of space constraints, such an overview is beyond the scope of this book. See below for recommended resources.

Our nation's current system utilizes local Workforce Development Boards (WDBs) to administer and coordinate workforce-development efforts in a region. We recommend that you contact your local WDB to discuss your interest in supporting local workforce development.[3] While you may not necessarily choose to work in an official partnership with your local WDB, it is a convenient way to understand the major actors and offerings in your area, helping refine your specific focus area.

In his CED handbook, Temali provides four basic questions to consider when developing a workforce-development program:

1. Which people will you serve, how will you recruit/get referrals and secure clients?

2. Which types of employers will you connect to?

3. Which types of services will you provide: preparation, training, placement, or retention support services?

3. See https://www.careeronestop.org/LocalHelp/WorkforceDevelopment/find-work force-development-boards.aspx for a WDB finder.

4. What approach: partnerships with other workforce-training organizations, partnerships with employers, comprehensive in-house program, or a contract with the local WDB?[4]

To this excellent list we add a fifth question; namely, how will your workforce-development program integrate with other CED strategies to provide a well-rounded, systematic effort to improve local economic prospects? For example, community benefits agreements (chapter 12) can provide funding for workforce development to prepare local residents for new employment opportunities associated with major new developments. Anchor institutions (chapter 11) can be vital partners, both as program funders and as potential employers for workforce-development participants. The work of business incubators (chapter 5), makerspaces (chapter 4), and cooperatives (chapter 6), when possible, should be tied directly into workforce development efforts to provide specific employment opportunities that contribute to overall community thriving.

Because of the sheer size and complexity of the workforce development system, it is critical, particularly for church-based CED efforts, to pinpoint a specific niche that is not being served effectively by the current system. You may determine that your highest value add is to improve access to existing services for certain members of your community such as single mothers, LEP immigrants, or those recently released from prison. To this end, preparation services such as soft-skills training and one-on-one coaching can give these individuals the confidence and connections to plug into the official workforce development system for further training and support.

If you decide to create your own niche offering that fits into the larger workforce development system, we recommend starting with the end in mind. That is, what specific employers will hire your clients, and what types of jobs will they be looking to fill? As mentioned above, integrating workforce development into other CED strategies that are creating employment opportunities can increase the impact of the overall CED effort. It is also critical to speak directly with local companies and engage them in designing and delivering your services. Research indicates that the most successful workforce-development programs are intimately tied to the local business community, particularly programs that focus on a specific industry sector.[5]

---

4. See chapter 6 in Temali, *Community Economic Handbook.*
5. Garmise, *Building a Workforce Development System.*

In one example from the research, a cluster of local manufacturing companies worked with a manufacturing-specific workforce-development program that served disadvantaged populations, delivering substantial savings compared to the old approach of using a temporary employment service. Close partnerships such as this can lead to employers as potential sources of funding for workforce-development programs. Businesses in such a system receive tremendous value because they are much more likely to have their specific needs fulfilled compared to utilizing generic employment agencies.

The Role of Churches

Aside from the obvious resource of space for workforce-development training and coaching sessions, a church's connections with the local community through its spiritual and social-outreach programs can be extremely valuable to a workforce-development program. This may be particularly true for individuals who for a variety of reasons may not feel comfortable visiting a training facility or employment agency with which they have no prior relationship. The church can provide a convenient and comfortable first stop, along with preparation services, towards full engagement with the local workforce-development system.

Depending on the size of your church, you may have business executives or human-resources managers in your congregation who can participate in an exploratory committee on workforce development. These voices can be instrumental in identifying a niche and getting the commitment of local employers to support a new workforce-development offering that simultaneously achieves CED objectives and delivers tangible business value to employers.

Depending on the size and scope of the workforce-development program, you may need volunteers to launch and operate it, particularly during the startup phase. While the program must be delivered in a professional, high-quality manner, churches can provide volunteers to help with tasks such as registration, intake, and support such as transportation or childcare. Some church members may also be qualified to participate as coaches or trainers.

Finally, churches can play a vital role as advocates for better workforce-development services for disadvantaged or marginalized communities and individuals. Becoming involved in your local WDB and calling attention to the challenges that your community members face can help ensure that the overall workforce-development system moves in a direction towards equity and improved impact for communities that need it most.

Challenges

As mentioned above, the complexity of the workforce development system is daunting. Working with established organizations or tapping into government funding may impose restrictions or structures on your ideal offering, driving you to consider a more independent route that can also be very challenging.

Successful workforce-development requires a functioning process from recruitment of participants to employment that is retained. For this reason, each of the five questions given above must receive full consideration and will require the development of a steering or advisory committee comprising potential participants, other service providers, church members, and employers. Partnerships should be guided not only by mutual interest in community thriving, but should also contain written agreements of understanding to clearly identify mutual expectations and handoffs between one organization and the next. Creating a tight process will not only be more efficient, it will help ensure that participants don't leak out of the system because of unclear next steps.

Finally, a number of factors contribute to an individual's employment prospects. Because CED-based programs often address gaps or shortfalls within the larger workforce-development system, the challenges can be more acute. Program objectives should be aggressive and not shy away from helping community members who may need the most help. However, this must be coupled with a realistic assessment of the role of workforce-development services in these potential clients. For example, helping community members without homes to achieve and maintain gainful employment will likely require coordination with housing services, addiction/recovery services, and other wrap-around services, without which workforce development services will likely not be effective.

Case Studies

UCOM

UCOM[6] is a ministry of the Michigan Conference of the United Church of Christ, located just outside of Grand Rapids, Michigan. Their program offers soft-skills training with a focus on helping especially hard-to-hire individuals such as ex-offenders. Partnerships with several area employers such as residential care facilities for seniors and targeting those with developmental disabilities provides a unique focus for this workforce-development program.

Harlem Congregations for Community Improvement Inc. (HCCI)

HCCI[7] is an interfaith coalition of congregations providing a wide range of economic-empowerment services in the Bradhurst area of central Harlem, including soft skills, literacy, resume writing, and computer training to support job placement. Their prior work in developing a large commercial/retail space anchored by a grocery store is also leveraged to provide employment pathways. In addition to providing direct services, HCCI is an example of a local organization that provides preparatory and referral services to connect their community members to services available within the local workforce-development system, including the area's WDB "Workforce 1."

Flourish Tech 206

A nonprofit associated with the now-closed Flourish Church Rainier Valley in the Seattle area, Flourish Tech 206[8] is hyper-focused on providing access for African Americans and other people of color to the world of cloud computing and technology sales. This endeavor reflects awareness of high-growth, high-paying jobs that are available in the area with an astute use of partnerships to provide the online training content and platform. While still in its infancy, this approach is a good example of finding a niche

6. https://www.ucomgr.org/work_skills.

7. https://www.hcci.org/untitled-lmjmw.

8. https://flourishtech206.com/.

and not getting bogged down trying to provide or coordinate too many pieces of the puzzle.

Further Reading and Exploration

Understanding Local Workforce Systems

An excellent report[9] by the Urban Institute to help readers understand the complex local workforce-development system, including organizations involved, populations served, and services provided. Includes guidance on learning more about your specific locale's system and questions to ask to assess its scope and impact.

Career One Stop: Find Training

A search engine to help in your audit of available workforce-development services in your area.[10]

Platform to Employment

Platform to Employment[11] is a proven program developed in Connecticut targeting the long-term unemployed, incorporating a comprehensive job-readiness program with training, workshops, and peer-to-peer support. Content is available in an online e-learning format. Includes an innovative eight-week trial period with potential employers during which the wage is subsidized by the workforce-development organization. The model is being replicated in several cities across the nation.

Cincinnati Works

A full-featured program centered on individualized coaching and strong connections to local employers. Their model is available for replication across the country.[12]

---

9. Eyster et al., *Understanding Local Workforce Systems.*

10. See https://www.careeronestop.org/FindTraining/find-training.aspx.

11. https://platformtoemployment.com/.

12. For more details, see https://cincinnatiworks.org/ or https://eliminatepoverty.org.

8

Commercial District Revitalization

Overview

YOUR COMMERCIAL DISTRICT IS typically the most noticeable area of your community, with more traffic and eyeballs than residential areas, industrial areas, and greenspaces. Improving your commercial district, or "Main Street," can be a highly visible, catalytic project that influences overall perceptions towards your community, draws new businesses, encourages residents to start or expand businesses, and provides jobs for existing residents. A vibrant commercial district can improve your community's quality of life by offering vital services within walking distance while functioning as a hub for community building. Most commercial district revitalization (CDR) programs comprise some combination of cleanup and beautification, building upgrades, business attraction, business support, and marketing to draw more consumers. Current best practice for such programs is to focus the revitalization on specific types of customers such as working-class residents or young families, or to focus on specific industries such as food, arts, retail, or health. And as we'll discuss below, a CDR strategy can be the cornerstone for a broad CED effort, providing focus for other CED programs such as microbusiness development (chapter 3), business incubators (chapter 5), and most of the other strategies discussed in this book.

However, there is also a potential dark side to CDR, with revitalization efforts at times encouraging or accelerating gentrification and displacement forces. Unless CDR is governed by a strong commitment to community, revitalized commercial districts can be a signal to outside businesses and non-residents that your neighborhood is an attractive place in which to invest, thereby driving up housing prices and driving out existing businesses and residents. In fact, many TED strategies incorporate CDR efforts, highlighting the need for accountable development interventions (chapter 12) to ensure that communities are not overrun by zealous TED efforts to improve commercial districts.

Nevertheless, CDR strategies are very popular, with around two-thousand organizations across the country following the so-called Main Street Approach,[1] along with many other locales pursuing *ad hoc* approaches and other methodologies.[2] The Main Street America organization has developed a field-tested methodology for CDR with technical assistance, educational resources, and a valuable community of practice. Their "Four Point" approach identifies the importance of organization, promotion, economic vitality, and design for all CDR initiatives, as described further in Table 2.

TABLE 2: MAIN STREET FOUR POINTS

Organization	Building organizational capacity for a sustainable revitalization effort, including cultivating partnerships, community involvement, and resources. Best practice recommendation is for a full-time director focused on the Main Street program, normally housed in a free-standing dedicated nonprofit, but can also be incorporated into CDCs or other community organizations.
Promotion	Positions the commercial district as the center of the community and hub of economic activity. Focus on creating a positive image rooted in a community's unique characteristics, encouraging engagement with both residents and non-residents.
Economic Vitality	Tools to assist new and existing businesses, including startup and growth capital, and incentives to relocate to the commercial district. Efforts to create a supportive environment for entrepreneurs and new business formation.
Design	Improvements to the built environment with building upgrades, landscaping, and other beautification efforts. Enhance walkability, access, and the overall aesthetic appeal of a commercial district.

1. http://www.mainstreet.org/.

2. See below for information on another popular methodology from LISC.

Temali includes CDR in his top four development strategies for communities to consider, identifying a total of thirteen different tools[3] that can be used in a CDR program:

1) cleanup campaign

2) partner with existing loan fund

3) operate own loan fund

4) grants for storefront improvement

5) storefront design

6) streetscape projects

7) business attraction efforts

8) marketing to consumers

9) address crime

10) learn lessons from shopping center management

11) parking development

12) real estate development

13) business improvement district

Getting Started

Identify Your Commercial District

The traditional view of "Main Street" is idyllic, with historic commercial buildings neatly lined next to each other, ample space for pedestrians, easy parking and public transportation, with a gazebo and fountain to top it off! In many communities, however, commercial activity is dispersed, some of it historic in nature, but with plenty of strip malls and areas of never-ending sprawl. It is critical to be very explicit about the geographic location of your proposed CDR efforts. Given the visual nature of CDR and its potential influence on perceptions towards the community, we recommend choosing a small, highly visible area where impact can be maximized. This may be a smaller, forgotten commercial corner rather than a full-blown district. The choice of location, of course, should be approached in conjunction with

3. Temali, *Community Economic Development Handbook*, ch. 4.

an overall assessment that examines community assets such as available buildings, as well as community desires to address problem areas that are abandoned and blighted.

Assessment

Revitalizing a commercial district is an attractive initial strategy for many CED efforts because it can produce visible results very quickly. CDR strategies can be approached incrementally, starting for example with fairly easy cleanup and streetscape projects such as the installation of banners, benches, or landscaping improvements. However, as with all CED strategies, we recommend you first engage in a thorough assessment process before embarking on such projects, ensuring that your initial small steps are part of a well thought out strategy that builds on community assets and meets real community economic needs.

The generic assessment process described in chapter 13 provides the basis for a CDR assessment. However, those seriously considering CDR should bolster this assessment by ensuring that the business inventory and outreach to existing and potential business owners is particularly robust. In addition, a CDR assessment should include some measure of buying power in the community, using tools such as Social Explorer[4] to examine residents' household spending patterns. A simple market analysis can then be performed to determine gaps in the current commercial district as weighed against the demand for such services by existing residents. Other considerations in assessing the need for a CDR strategy include the prevalence of vacant properties or buildings in the commercial district, the financial health of current businesses, how quickly new businesses fill up empty space, how frequently residents utilize the commercial district for shopping, and whether the district functions well as a community hub.

It is very common for analysis, and simple observation, to reveal a need for more businesses in your commercial district. You should determine the capacity of your community to generate those businesses through microbusiness development (chapter 3), business incubators (chapter 5), and the development of cooperatives (chapter 6). If your community lacks such programs, you must consider the relative importance of CDR versus first improving the capacity of your community to generate new businesses. While this may pose a chicken-and-egg dilemma, possible solutions are to

4. See chapter 13 for an overview of this powerful data visualization tool.

partner with other organizations to bring these needed business-creation services to your community, or jumpstart CDR efforts by attracting new businesses from outside of the community. Of course, this raises the specter of gentrification and displacement as mentioned above, a topic that will be covered in more detail when challenges are discussed below.

Coalition Building

As described in Table 2, the Main Street Approach recommends the creation of a dedicated, standalone nonprofit to spearhead CDR efforts, along with a full-time director. Such steps will likely be difficult for most churches to attempt during the early stages of involvement with CED, highlighting the importance of creating a strong coalition of supporters and participants, particularly for CDR efforts. Starting with strong support and growing your coalition as small-scale improvements to the commercial district are achieved can pave the way for a dedicated nonprofit to be established along with the resources to hire a full-time director.

Create a Shared Vision

A strong coalition of supporters will enable you to create a shared vision for the commercial district. Unless your church has already engaged in programs in which a shared community vision was successfully created, we heartily recommend partnering with an existing CDC or other community organization that has an established community outreach process and has already established its credibility in the community. Establishing a vision for your commercial district may be contentious. For example, how can the diverse nature of a community be represented in a commercial district's look and feel, and what types of businesses are most desired? Some stakeholders may want to focus on attracting new investments and customers from other communities, while others will want to maintain or reestablish connections with the history of the community.

Action Planning

Once the vision for the commercial district is established, develop an action plan to identify and prioritize Temali's thirteen tools to work together in a coordinated and strategic manner. How these plans come together will vary dramatically from community to community. The plan should also include preliminary ideas for complementary CED programs as discussed above.

You may be daunted at this stage by the endless range of possibilities for CDR. Fortunately, the Main Street organization has developed a number of pre-packaged "Catalyst Strategies" that are oriented around a particular focus or vision for a commercial district. While these strategies do not in any way reduce the importance of a robust assessment as described above, they can help communities coalesce more quickly around a shared vision. Two types of strategies are provided: those based on certain targeted customers (such as "Workers and Residents," "Millennials," or "Family Friendly"), and those focused on a specific industry or product (such as "Apparel," "Food," or "Health and Wellness").

The Role of Churches

Churches can support CDR efforts in a wide variety of ways, ranging from providing volunteers for cleanup and beautification events, to funding and spinning off a dedicated nonprofit. Churches with endowments or wealthy members can consider funding loan and grant programs to help existing commercial district businesses expand or make storefront improvements, as well as help new businesses with startup and move-in costs.

In some communities, what is needed is somebody to make the first move by renting or purchasing a vacant building and developing it. As described in the case study below, churches can lead or catalyze such efforts, drawing on endowment funds or bringing together investors around a vision of revitalization. Such efforts can include starting a business in the revamped space as well as attracting new businesses to utilize the space.

You may find that your church is located in or very near to a commercial district. In these cases, churches can take advantage of their buildings, property, or parking lots, to support CDR. Buildings can be repurposed to include operations, manufacturing, or storage space for businesses, and empty land can be turned into open-air markets, food cart pods, or parks, to help draw more customers to a commercial district. Parking lots can be allocated for commercial district use to ease parking burdens, potentially even including a shuttle service to make things easier for those who need it. See the appendix for more on the exciting possibilities for "reimagining religious spaces."

In addition to these many practical ways to support CDR, perhaps the most important role for a church is to help keep the focus on those who are marginalized in the community. Even if your church does not have the resources to directly invest in CDR, you can participate in coalition building and ensure that all stakeholders within a community are being heard and are involved in crafting the shared vision for the commercial district.

Challenges

A significant challenge for those pursuing a CDR strategy is rooted in the classic community-development dilemma of the "inside game" versus the "outside game."[5] That is, does real change in urban communities require regional solutions through integration with the larger regional economy (the outside game), or can place-based efforts centered on directly strengthening struggling communities lift them out of poverty (the inside game)? This is related to a core theory in economic development, the so-called economic base theory, which states that economic growth requires demand from *outside* of a community or region and that communities cannot thrive based solely on community-serving businesses. These theories present themselves in CDR as a choice between emphasizing community-oriented businesses that cater to the needs of existing residents, or "destination businesses" that may appeal to both residents and those outside of the community. As CED proponents, we recommend an emphasis on the former with carefully managed introductions of the latter. We agree with the basic economic principle that an influx of capital from outside of the community can be good for local economies, but only if it is managed carefully. Even businesses that may appeal to those outside of the community, however, should reinforce and support the shared vision for the community in general and the commercial district specifically. Mismanaging this aspect of CDR could result in unleashing gentrification and displacement forces.

A second challenge is that, in many cities, there will already be one or more CDR efforts underway. While these initiatives may be driven by community-oriented nonprofits, it is equally likely that they are sponsored and managed by local or regional governmental economic-development agencies as a component of a broader TED initiative. If these TED efforts impinge on the commercial district within your community, you will be hard pressed to pursue your own CDR strategy, given the sizeable budgets

5. See Imbroscio, *Shaming the Inside Game.*

and support by community elites that such TED initiatives typically enjoy. In these cases, you may be forced to play defense and seek to leverage the dollars invested in these CDR efforts while protecting the interests of your overall community. Chapter 12 provides an extensive discussion on accountable development which will likely be required in these scenarios.

Case Study: Mosaic and 72204

Mark DeYmaz is an entrepreneurial church planter and recognized leader of the multiethnic church movement in the United States. In 2001, Mark planted Mosaic in the 72204 zip code of Little Rock, Arkansas, a high-crime, high-poverty area that other evangelical churches had eschewed. His inspirational and groundbreaking work over the last twenty years is chronicled well in his book *Disruption*,[6] so here we just mention a few of the highlights as they pertain to CDR. The "commercial district" that Mark ended up working in was an 80,000 square foot former Walmart building that had been vacant for eight years. When Mark's unrealistic offer to rent the building from Walmart for $650 a month was accepted, his church moved into the massive building, roof leaks included, and the positive community impacts began almost immediately. For example, the parking lot was no longer a drug infested crime haven, and crime within a one mile radius dropped by an incredible 12.3 percent. A number of businesses moved into sections of the massive building over the next several years, providing sorely needed jobs and retail services to the surrounding community. When their lease with Walmart converted to a month-to-month arrangement, Mark started to pray and look for a permanent home for Mosaic, one in which the church could operate as a benevolent owner.

The opportunity came when they were able to purchase an old Kmart building. Over the next several years, the church secured the purchase of the property as well as a long-term tenant, 10 Fitness. This arrangement not only provided Mosaic with an income stream that essentially covered the mortgage on the property, the improvements that 10 Fitness made increased the value of the property by over $2 million. Space for small businesses such as food trucks was made available and the property continues to bless the local economy. The work of Mosaic in 72204 has garnered a tremendous amount of attention and admiration from the surrounding

---

6. DeYmaz, *Disruption*.

community, culminating in receiving the 2016 Economic Development Award from the Arkansas Martin Luther King, Jr. Commission.[7]

Further Reading and Exploration

Main Street America

The previously mentioned Main Street America[8] is a critical resource for those considering CDR. While non-members can access a number of resources, membership is required in order to access the full range of benefits. Their Urban Main program[9] has been developed for CDR in under-resourced communities, with consideration of the unique challenges facing these communities such as lack of funding and gentrification pressures.

Commercial Revitalization Planning Guide

The national intermediary LISC has created a model to guide CDR efforts, backed by years of experience in working with communities across the nation. Their Commercial Revitalization Planning Guide[10] is a particularly robust, freely available resource that is highly recommended for those considering CDR.

7. For a complete account, you are encouraged to read chapter five of DeYmaz, *Disruption*.

8. See www.mainstreet.org.

9. See https://www.urbanmain.org/.

10. See Jacobus and Maureen, *Commercial Revitalization Planning Guide*.

9

Good Jobs Focus

Overview

THIS CHAPTER LOOKS AT explicitly increasing the supply of good jobs available to community residents, recognizing that while getting a job is good, not all jobs are "good jobs." Using a good-jobs lens can influence how you approach a variety of CED programs, as well as open possibilities for new types of programs. We have already delved into a variety of strategies to produce jobs such as microbusiness support (chapter 3), makerspaces (chapter 4), business incubation (chapter 5), worker cooperatives (chapter 6), and commercial-district revitalization (chapter 8). These are vital and necessary approaches in most communities. However, the reality is that in self-employment and small-business scenarios, it can be quite difficult to get past the precarious startup stage to a period of stable revenue generation. Unfortunately, many of these ventures will fail or remain small, with the most successful providing modest wealth generation for the founder(s) and a stable paycheck for a small handful of employees. While a successful commercial district can provide larger levels of employment for community residents, these jobs are typically skewed towards retail and service, with low pay and minimal benefits. Workforce development (chapter 7) programs are another piece of the employment puzzle, but even the best of these programs will fail if there is not an adequate supply of jobs, particularly good jobs, for residents to be hired into.

Typically, a good-jobs focus is not a standalone CED program. To be most effective, it should weave together a number of CED strategies to

(1) nurture and expand current sources of good jobs, (2) create new opportunities for good jobs, and (3) prepare and connect community residents to those jobs. Note that while these efforts can and should include support for local living-wage ordinances, the primary focus of this chapter is working directly with businesses to provide good jobs. More information on policy interventions and advocacy efforts is provided near the end of this chapter.

Finally, we must make a distinction between TED efforts to attract businesses that promise lots of "good jobs" and a CED approach that seeks to increase the supply of such jobs to directly benefit marginalized or under-resourced communities. Chapter 12 will discuss the pitfalls of these TED business-attraction efforts, calling for accountable-development interventions such as community benefits agreements to ensure that the promised jobs materialize and that community members are actually hired into these good jobs.

Getting Started

Defining a "Good Job"

While the definition of a good job is highly personal and culturally contingent, we propose three primary characteristics:

1. *Pays a living wage*: rather than tying target wages to highly variable and inadequate minimum-wage laws, the living-wage movement advocates for individuals and families to make enough to meet minimum standards for living in their specific locale. A "Living Wage Calculator," updated annually, is available from MIT[1] to determine a living wage for individuals as well as those with children, by state, county, and metropolitan geographies. An alternative approach looks at wages necessary to achieve self-sufficiency, taking into account family size, ages of children, and geographic differences.[2]

2. *Benefits*: health insurance and sick pay are particularly valuable and necessary given our country's high healthcare costs and the risks of medically related financial hardship or bankruptcy.

3. *Stability*: Regular and predictable work hours to enable financial planning and budgeting, as well as scheduling for childcare and other life activities.

1. See https://livingwage.mit.edu/.
2. See http://www.selfsufficiencystandard.org/.

Other characteristics for a good job are certainly possible and should be considered based on input from your community. While the definition you choose should be clear and somewhat aspirational, it should also be realistic. Not all jobs in your community will meet your definition, with some minimum-wage jobs being perhaps necessary to build workforce experience for some members of your community. The key is to create a clear distinction between these minimum-wage jobs and the good jobs that should be the true goal for community job growth and workforce-development efforts.

Assessment

A CED focus on good jobs must be realistic, centered on current community assets in the form of anchor institutions, existing businesses, and available workforce. For example, attracting or supporting the start of a new supermarket or small manufacturer may be a viable CED approach to produce good jobs. However, creating a brand-new cluster of high-tech firms paying six-figure incomes is likely unrealistic. Using the assessment process outlined in chapter 13, we recommend a focus on identifying current businesses in and near your community that provide good jobs. Based on a survey of residents, identify the primary "good job" employers for community residents, keeping in mind that not all of these businesses will be physically located in your community. Assuming they are within reasonable commute distances and on convenient public transportation lines, these employers should be considered to be within the employment sphere of your community. Your assessment of residents should also look for hard-to-hires such as those with felony records, immigrants with minimal English language skills, or those in recovery. In such groups, even those who are employed are likely to be stuck in low-wage jobs with limited chances to get into good jobs. Such findings can help focus your good jobs strategy on those within your community who could benefit the most.

Following our recommended assessment process will also create a building/property inventory and identify current economic exchanges such as commercial districts or marketplaces that may provide opportunities for business expansion. Identifying anchor institutions (chapter 11), particularly those with a commitment to localized purchasing, is also critical to identify opportunities for the growth of good jobs. Ultimately, the goal for this assessment is to identify critical community assets around which to build a good jobs focus. Below we identify three potential strategies to consider pursing.

Strategic Options

Help Current Businesses Expand

Based on your assessment, which employers are currently providing good jobs for your community's residents? Creating more opportunities for such jobs can be achieved by creating a specialized workforce-development program (chapter 7) that prepares community residents to acquire and keep jobs at these employers. Such programs can be a valuable source of competitive advantage for employers by saving them recruitment and training costs as well as nurturing a consistent supply of well-qualified, local employees. Another approach is to help these existing businesses expand and create more jobs. The barriers to expansion will vary, of course, calling for well-rounded business accelerator programs[3] providing loans, technical assistance, and other services. In some cases, businesses may need affordable space to fuel their expansion. This will require creative deal making in which available community assets such as empty commercial real estate or underutilized church space are made available with attractive leasing terms in exchange for the production of more good jobs. As called for in accountable development (chapter 12), we recommend formalizing such arrangements with written legal agreements clearly stipulating expectations for both parties, along with monitoring and enforcement provisions.

Attract or Start a New Business

In many communities, there will already be TED programs to attract new businesses or even new industries to a metropolitan area. As discussed in chapter 12, these deals are often controversial and must be negotiated and monitored diligently to ensure that benefits accrue to the communities and people who need it the most. While we do not recommend mimicking such approaches at a CED level, there are cases where attracting a new business into the community can be a valuable component of an overall

3. Although chapter 5 focuses primarily on the closely related concept of business incubation, information on strategies to help businesses expand through accelerator services is also covered briefly.

CED program. For example, many lower-income communities lack basic community-serving businesses such as supermarkets, creating food deserts that drive up the costs of food and negatively impact community health outcomes. Convincing an established grocer to move into the community, or starting such a business, can be a tremendous boon to a community and catalyze further economic-development activity.

However, we must recognize the challenges facing such an endeavor, as witnessed by the very fact that such a private business does not currently exist in your community. A concerted CED effort to bring in or start such a business in the community can help overcome some of the barriers holding private investment back, turning the investment into an attractive opportunity with acceptable risk. For example, a CED effort can organize and amplify community support, advocate for needed zoning or land-use changes, broker attractive rent on space, or help fund needed building upgrades and capital expansion through loans and grants. Pursuing a commercial-district revitalization program (chapter 8) in tandem can also sweeten the deal for businesses considering locating into your community. Finally, a specialized, dedicated workforce-development program, as described above, can also positively impact the risk/reward calculation to start such a business in your community.

Good Jobs through Anchor Institutions

Our third and final strategic option for good jobs taps anchor institutions such as hospitals, universities, or museums. As prime sources of good jobs, CED can develop and offer specialized workforce-development programs to increase the number of community residents who work for anchor institutions. Second, anchor institutions committed to local procurement can help form a cluster of supplier businesses in your community, with strong commitments to not only meet cost and quality levels for the anchor institution, but to provide good jobs to community residents. See chapter 11 for a complete discussion on leveraging anchor institutions for CED.

The Role of Churches

Churches can support good jobs by organizing living-wage ordinance and related employment advocacy efforts at local, state, and even national levels. For example, you can draw awareness to the struggles of residents who may be employed in minimum-wage jobs and ensure their voices are being heard. Churches that lead or participate in other CED programs such as workforce development (chapter 7), commercial district revitalization (chapter 8), and accountable development (chapter 12), can push for a commitment in these programs beyond "any job," setting targets instead for "good jobs." As with many other CED strategies, churches should also seek out those forgotten or neglected corners of the community, advocating for hard-to-hires and even developing targeted workforce development programs to open more opportunities for good jobs to these groups.

Some churches will have members who are already successful business owners. Teaching and nurturing the adoption of a robust theology of work (see chapter 1) can encourage business owners to apply their faith to hiring, promotion, and compensation practices. When coupled with other CED programs such as a church-supported workforce development program, the impact on community thriving can be truly remarkable. See the case study section below for an example.

Churches can reduce the financial risks for new businesses that provide good jobs to locate into their community through the provision of space, whether in the form of buildings, property, or even parking lots. In some cases, churches can leverage their own real estate assets or take the lead in purchasing and developing an abandoned building.[4] Finally, churches can also pull together community and church resources to start a new business, spinning it off as a separate for-profit or nonprofit business that is committed to serving the community through its products/services as well as being a source of good jobs.

Challenges

Which comes first, the good job or the local resident qualified to fill that good job? This dilemma captures the challenge of CED to work on both the supply of jobs and the supply of a qualified workforce. As covered in chapter 7's discussion on workforce development, strong ties to the business community are required in order to ensure that program graduates meet current employer demands, with the most successful programs delivering tangible business value to their partner businesses. This is even more critical when the employers are being asked to provide jobs delivering a living wage, benefits, and other good-jobs characteristics.

4. See the Mosaic case study in chapter 8 for an example.

In some industries, it is standard practice to offer good jobs, while in others, such as retail or fast-food, it is relatively rare. Finding business owners and managers committed to providing good jobs is more challenging than simply filling a space with any business ready to pay the rent. This may require putting together a business case for skeptical business owners, showing the overall benefits of providing good jobs. Research indicates that paying a living wage can lead to reduced turnover, improved morale, and increased productivity that can save employers literally thousands of dollars. Further, the overall health of the community's economy will increase as more residents are employed in good jobs, with the increased wages providing more discretionary income for residents to spend at local businesses. A commitment to provide retention-oriented workforce development programs (see chapter 7) can also contribute to reduced turnover and help make the business case for good jobs. The reality is, however, that a CED focus on good jobs may require you to be pickier about the businesses that you seek to attract and support.

Case Study: CityUnite Work Matters

CityUnite Work Matters[5] is a faith-oriented collaboration in the Denver metropolitan area that unites faith, business, and government around the common good. The Work Matters program works specifically with businesses to help them invest in their communities. The example of L&R Pallet, a successful, medium-sized, second-generation business, highlights the special impact of businesses committed to providing good jobs to marginalized populations. Through targeted hiring, a commitment to good jobs, and support services for newly landed Burmese refugees, L&R Pallet has seen turnover drop from 300 percent to an astoundingly low 5 percent, removing one of the primary barriers to growth that the company was facing.[6] The CityUnite website provides this and several other video case studies that can help cast a vision for your good-jobs efforts and the businesses with whom you are working.

5. https://cityunite.org/work-matters/.
6. See the video case study, CityUnite, "Place of Refuge."

Further Reading and Exploration

Business Cases and Economic Impacts of Living Wages

*Ton, "Raising Wages Is the Right Thing to Do, and Doesn't
Have to Be Bad for Your Bottom Line."*

This short article[7] from Harvard Business Review highlights the positive business impacts for companies paying living wages. A book-length treatment is also available in Zeynep Ton's book entitled *The Good Jobs Strategy.*[8]

Chapman and Thompson, "The Economic Impact of Local Living Wages."

This extensive report[9] from the Economic Policy Institute examines the positive impact of living wages on local economies, consumers, workers, and businesses.

Good Jobs and Accountable Development

GoodJobsFirst.org

This policy-oriented website[10] provides many resources to support a good-jobs strategy, particularly at the intersection with accountable development (chapter 12).

Partnership for Working Families: Living Wage

An online resource[11] for those advocating for living-wage ordinances, including incorporation of living-wage policies into community benefits agreements.

---

7. Ton, "Raising Wages Is the Right Thing to Do."
8. Ton, *Good Jobs Strategy.*
9. Chapman and Thompson, "Economic Impact of Local Living Wages."
10. See https://www.goodjobsfirst.org.
11. See the resources page at https://www.forworkingfamilies.org/.

Theology of Work and Good Jobs

Denver Institute for Faith and Work

The Denver Institute nonprofit[12] works with many different companies to encourage the higher calling of faith expressed through work. Their site provides numerous case studies and articles highlighting the positive business, community, and faith impacts of good jobs in faith-shaped businesses.

12. See https://denverinstitute.org/learn/good-jobs-poverty/.

10

Locality Development: Housing and Land Use

Overview

BECAUSE LAND IS ONE of the most valuable assets in a community, it has tremendous potential to contribute to overall community economic prosperity. However, land has often been used in TED as a tool to enrich the haves and erode the prospects for the have nots. Demolition of neighborhoods in the name of urban "renewal," replacement of affordable housing with luxury condominiums, single-family zoning and anti-density biases, under investment and divestment in communities of color, all have contributed to the ubiquitous place-based inequality described in chapter 1. "Locality development" is an umbrella term that encompasses transportation planning, urban design, and the overall regulation and management of the land and buildings in a community.[1] From an economic development perspective, locality development significantly impacts a community's prospects for economic growth based on its amenities, walkability, safety, and "look and feel" attributes. This chapter will focus on how land and buildings can contribute to the goals of CED, focusing on areas that are particularly relevant to faith-based CED including community land trusts and affordable housing on church property. Since locality development comprises many topics, each large enough to have a literal book written on them, the Further Reading and Exploration section at the end of the chapter is particularly robust and important.

---

1. Leigh and Blakely, *Planning Local Economic Development*, 231.

The scale of locality development matters tremendously: decisions made to optimize region- or city-wide outcomes can have devastating consequences for specific neighborhoods. History is replete with examples of how land use and planning driven by TED principles of efficiency and economic growth have decimated local economies, particularly in communities of color, all in the name of regional economic progress.[2] For example, interstate freeways built through metropolitan areas across the nation in the second half of the last century were utterly destructive for many local communities and local economies. Today, as neighborhood roads are expanded into regional arterials, we witness similar negative impacts on local economies, with walkability and easy access to local businesses sacrificed for an "improved regional transportation infrastructure." Organizing to oppose such development, while typically thought of in terms of community development, clearly fits into an overall CED strategy because of the implications for local economies. Accountable development (chapter 12), in conjunction with community benefits agreements (CBAs), provides a natural point of intersection between CED and the broader concerns of locality development. CBAs can help ensure that large development projects that impact land use, such as commercial developments, transportation projects, or corporate expansions, bring benefits to marginalized communities and people.

Community land trusts (CLTs) provide local communities with a mechanism to maintain control over property as a community asset. CLTs enable the community, through a representative board, to make decisions on how to use land to serve community thriving instead of leaving it to the vagaries of market forces or political whims. CLTs separate ownership of land from ownership of buildings, using long-term ground leases along with restrictions on resale of buildings to maintain affordability in perpetuity. In most cases, a separate nonprofit is established to raise funds, procure properties, and manage the portfolio. While CLTs are normally associated with residential housing, the mechanism can be applied to any type of land use including commercial space, community parks, or any other uses the community decides are most needed. In cases where the community has vacant or underutilized property, the acquired property can be banked for future uses or adapted immediately to meet current community needs.

Aside from land, housing is perhaps the most critical type of community asset within the purview of locality development, dictating residential

---

2. See for example Jackson, *Crabgrass Frontier*; Rothstein, *Color of Law*.

composition, business location decisions, neighborhood stability, and overall quality of life. As housing goes, so goes the neighborhood, with a community's economic trajectory tied directly to this valuable community asset. As forces such as gentrification sweep through metropolitan areas, neighborhoods are upended as affordability plummets and those with lower incomes are forced to move to less desirable, but more affordable, neighborhoods. Those who manage to stay spend an increasing percentage of their income on housing, leaving less for discretionary spending at local businesses, while others are forced to draw on social services to make ends meet. In its most dramatic and visible form, homelessness increases as affordable housing options disappear. In some communities, community development has become synonymous with housing development, as CDCs and other community groups focus exclusively on protecting and developing housing for its lower-income residents.

Unfortunately, many cities fail to recognize the economic importance of providing housing for all community residents until a crisis such as homelessness starts to visibly impinge on business and overall economic growth. Typical TED responses reinforce inequality, with many municipalities effectively creating economic ghettos by pushing affordable housing development to the outskirts. However, CED is not content with economic growth at the cost of displacing existing residents. CED recognizes that affordable housing is an important contributor to community thriving for *all*. The economic benefits of an equitable housing strategy are myriad, including: (1) vibrant, diverse, mixed-income communities; (2) reduced housing cost burdens with more community members contributing to the local economy through goods and services purchased from earned wages; (3) affordable-housing homeownership programs leading to increased community wealth and neighborhood stability; and (4) increases to the local tax base through productive, taxable use of vacant or underutilized properties.

Getting Started

Community Land Trusts

Starting a CLT is a large undertaking. If your metropolitan area already has a CLT, you should consider working with them before deciding to start a separate CLT. Making the decision to create a new CLT or partner with an existing one will depend on your CED goals and the focus of existing CLTs in your community. John Emmeus Davis provides a useful set of organizing questions that are crucial to frame this decision process:

1. *Why?* There are myriad potential benefits of a CLT, but here the foundational question is how the CLT will further your CED goals. CLTs can be used as a tool to fight against gentrification-induced displacement. They can support an affordable-housing initiative to address homelessness or be used to increase homeownership rates. CLTs can "bank" land for the community to give the community more control over its future. *Why (or how) will a CLT further your CED goals?*

2. *Who/Where?* A closely related question is who will your CLT serve or benefit? Who will ultimately live on or use the land? For housing-oriented CLTs, a key question is the target income level for owners or renters. Since most CED efforts are focused on specific neighborhoods, your CLT will likely have a geographic focus, and possibly even a finer-grained focus such as supporting immigrants or people of color. *Who will your CLT serve and where will its focus be?*

3. *Constituents?* As with most of the strategies in this book, building a coalition of supporters is critical. Davis highlights five constituencies that should be engaged at the onset of considering a CLT: (1) community individuals and institutions, (2) other nonprofits serving the community and target population, (3) local government, (4) potential lenders and donors, and (5) housing development professionals. During this initial outreach, you may discover support and assets that can significantly impact the direction of the CLT. For example, an anchor institution (chapter 11) may be interested in being a CLT sponsor and funder, or local governments may be interested in procuring and leasing out vacant or abandoned properties for CLT usage.[3]

Whether you decide to start a new CLT or partner with an existing one, another critical issue is how you will build your initial portfolio of properties. As you reach out to constituents, you should look for initial property from multiple potential sources, including: (1) donated property from individuals interested in leaving a legacy to the community, (2) donated church property such as an unused field, parking lot, or other underutilized asset, (3) municipalities with abandoned or vacated property willing to sell or give the property to a CLT, (4) foundations providing grants to procure

3. Davis, *Starting a Community Land Trust.*

property, (5) property sold at below-market or donated to a CLT as a condition of a community benefits agreement with a private developer, and (6) anchor institutions with unused or underutilized property.

Affordable Housing

Affordable housing is a very large topic, with many options to consider: types of housing (single-family or multi-family), ownership structures (traditional ownership, rental, mutual housing, cooperatives), program focus areas (new development, retrofitting/remodeling, home maintenance support, sweat-equity builds, community and resident services, advocacy), and development strategy (establish a new development corporation or partner with an existing one). Affordable housing can also be combined with CLTs to provide for perpetually affordable housing.

In most metropolitan areas, there are likely already multiple active affordable-housing developers, both nonprofit and for-profit. However, even with so many developers, it is equally likely that your community still lacks affordable housing. In one sense, *any* new affordable housing is a welcome development, but as a component of a CED strategy, affordable housing should be developed with a specific economic development focus in mind. The following questions can help organize and focus your efforts within the immense space of possibilities:

1. *What are your economic development objectives?* Some possible objectives include: (1) increase the rate of homeownership in your community; (2) provide workforce housing, both rental and to own, to enable workers to live close to jobs; (3) reduce gentrification-induced displacement by providing existing residents more options to rent or own; (4) provide rental housing and services for the lowest rungs of the income ladder to address homelessness.

2. *Geographic focus area?* Presumably your overall CED strategy will have a geographic focus already established. In addition to this you must consider where land or buildings may be available for new affordable-housing projects, where your target residents live, and where your target residents work. Proximity to amenities such as parks, bike lanes, and transit stops should also be considered, as well as the walkability score for residents without an automobile.

3. *Target residents?* As with other CED strategies, you should ask who is being left behind or falling through the cracks of existing programs. Examples include: (1) low-income immigrants who are newly arrived to the country, (2) the "working poor" who are increasingly not able to afford living in their neighborhood, and (3) low-wage earners forced to commute long distances to newly created jobs associated with new commercial or municipal development.

One particularly intriguing trend in affordable housing is an increase in development on church property. As part of a larger trend of reimagining religious spaces (see the appendix), churches across the country are taking advantage of their valuable properties such as vacant fields, large parking lots, or underutilized buildings, to provide affordable housing to their community. The opportunity in most metropolitan areas is very large, with estimates of 600 (Portland, OR),[4] 3,000 (San Antonio),[5] and 5,000 (Denver region)[6] acres of church land available for affordable housing development. Significant challenges exist, however. Since these church-based projects are often smaller than the fifty unit minimum size for standard affordable-housing development, it can be difficult to get the interest of affordable-housing developers. Competing for traditional sources of capital, especially low-income housing tax credits (LIHTC), will be difficult when running up against larger projects going after the same funds. Navigating the complex worlds of real estate development, land-use regulations, and financing is also a challenge for most church leaders, although such expertise is likely available within the church membership. Zoning and land-use regulations also typically need modification to facilitate such development, requiring advocacy and organizing efforts. Finally, building support in the neighborhood surrounding the church and overcoming NIMBYism (Not-In-My-Back-Yard-ism) requires relationship building, education, and perseverance.

Fortunately, several organizations across the country have pioneered efforts to help congregations interested in developing affordable housing on their property. The Portland-based Leaven Community Land & Housing Coalition[7] has developed a cohort-based process to guide interested

---

4. Tannler, "Removing Regulatory Barriers to Development."

5. Dimmick, "City Offers Help to Churches."

6. Kenney, "Denver Has a Housing Crisis."

7. https://www.leaven.org/land-housing-organizing.

congregations in discernment and discovery, pre-development activities, and support in hiring a development partner. Making Housing & Community Happen is an organization located in Pasadena, California, with extensive experience in church-based affordable housing. They provide a number of resources including learning institutes and assistance in developing on church property. See the case study section below for more information on both of these organizations.

The Role of Churches

In addition to providing land for affordable-housing development, churches have several critical functions to play in affordable housing. At the broadest level, churches can organize and advocate for accountable development (chapter 12) to address pressures that may be contributing to the affordable housing crisis in their community. Faith communities can work together to pressure local government officials to fund more affordable housing, as well as to change zoning and land use regulations to be more supportive of affordable-housing development. Making Housing & Community Happen provides a good model for this type of local advocacy work.[8]

NIMBYism is a typical challenge for affordable-housing efforts. Churches can help soften this effect, first by solidifying internal support through preaching and teaching on affordable housing as an issue of justice.[9] The surrounding community can be reached through long-term relationship development as well as hosting community educational events on various topics related to affordable housing. Parish-oriented churches that remove the distinction between "church" and "community" are in the strongest positions to fight against these forces of NIMBYism.

Wrap-around or supportive housing services are also key areas for churches to further the affordable-housing cause. In many cases, churches are already involved in a variety of social-service ministries that can be adapted to meet the needs of residents of affordable housing, such as affordable childcare, financial training and assistance, transportation assistance, addiction and recovery treatment. Other CED strategies such as workforce development (chapter 7) can help renters and new homeowners with employment stability and security, representing another avenue for churches to support affordable housing.

8. https://www.makinghousinghappen.org/congregational-land.

9. For an excellent framing of affordable housing as justice, see Shook, *Making Housing Happen*.

For churches directly pursuing housing development, many opportunities exist to engage with the resources present in church members. For example, architects, builders, developers, and financiers can all apply their God-given skills towards church-based affordable housing development. Even if these individuals don't participate professionally in the development activities, they can be valuable members of steering committees, particularly during the process of vetting potential development partners.

Finally, churches can donate unused or underutilized property to help seed new CLTs. In cases where the church property is aligned with the CLTs geographic and land-use focus area, the donated property can be used directly for development. In other cases, the property could potentially be sold, with the proceeds used to procure other property for incorporation into the CLT. Congregations with aging members could also institute a program to encourage estate donations of property or money to church-based CLTs.

Challenges

In addition to the specific challenges discussed above, perhaps the biggest challenge for CED with respect to locality development is where to focus amidst all of the possibilities. While we have recommended several focus areas oriented around CLTs and affordable housing, your specific context may warrant a different focus. In many cases, good accountable development (chapter 12) will serve to turn potential negative developments into positive developments, but such interventions are unfortunately reactive in nature, dependent on large new development projects in your area. More proactive efforts that improve neighborhood walkability, increase access to parks and greenspaces, or beautify landscapes and streetscapes may be more appropriate as first steps for locality development in your community.

Extended timeframes could also be a challenge for both CLTs and affordable housing efforts. Establishing a CLT takes time, and even after you procure property, the entire development process must still unfold. Affordable housing is also a long-term project, requiring several years from conception to completion. If your community or organization needs to see some quicker CED wins, you should probably look elsewhere. Maturing your CED efforts to the point where you have a portfolio of strategies on varying timeframes should be your goal, opening up opportunities to address strategies such as those discussed in this chapter that may take several years or longer to see tangible results.

Case Studies

Leaven Community & Housing Coalition

This previously mentioned coalition[10] of congregations in Portland, Oregon, provides an excellent example of tenacity, collaboration, and passion for God's love of justice. Birthed from a vision to build affordable housing on the property of Portsmouth Union Church[11] in North Portland, five-plus years of efforts have resulted in zoning regulation changes, the creation of a city-faith community liaison to make these types of projects easier in the future, and a $2.3 million grant to begin development of a 20-unit affordable housing complex on their property. The coalition has developed a cohort-based process to help many other congregations listen, research, and act, in community with likeminded congregations across the Portland metropolitan region. They have captured their learnings in the form of a guide entitled "Discerning Whether Your Faith Community Should Build Affordable Housing: Process Guide & Technical Manual."[12]

Making Housing & Community Happen

This organization[13] in Pasadena, California, has been on the forefront of faith-based affordable housing for many years. The founder, Jill Shook, has edited a book (see below) that is essential reading for those interested in pursuing this route. The organization is particularly notable for its work in local advocacy, with its "Greater Pasadena Affordable Housing Group" hosting monthly housing-justice forums and guiding sub-committees to tackle a variety of policy-oriented issues to improve availability of affordable housing for all. The organization has also developed a specific process to guide congregations interested in developing affordable housing on their land.[14]

10. https://www.leaven.org/land-housing-organizing.

11. https://portsmouthunionchurch.org/affordable-housing.

12. Leaven Community & Housing Coalition, *Discerning Whether Your Faith Community Should Build Affordable Housing*.

13. https://www.makinghousinghappen.org.

14. For more examples, see https://www.housingfinance.com/developments/blessed-homes_0, https://cbehnke.wixsite.com/maximizingmission/affordable-housing, and https://faithandleadership.com/affordable-housing-rises-where-church-building-once-stood.

Further Reading and Exploration

General Locality Development

Congress for the New Urbanism (CNU)

CNU is an organization and movement centered on championing walkable, just, resilient, people-centered places. See their resources tab for an extensive list of books on a variety of relevant subjects. Many local chapters exist, including a Christian Caucus.[15]

The Space Between: A Christian Engagement with the Built Environment

This book[16] by Eric O. Jacobsen provides a theology of place that incorporates justice and flourishing from a Christian perspective. Helps readers to think theologically about the built environment.

Community Land Trusts

Community-Wealth.org CLT resource center

A valuable online collection[17] of information on CLTs including historic background, research, best practices, and a useful getting started guide[18] by John Emmeus Davis.

Grounded Solutions Network

A training and education oriented nonprofit working in the areas of affordable housing and CLTs.[19] The organization provides online training on a number of topics such as their CLT Startup Hub, with links to many resources including a CLT Technical Manual, business planning worksheets, examples, and more.

---

15. See https://www.center4eleadership.org/cnu-members-christian-caucus.
16. Jacobsen, *Space Between*.
17. https://community-wealth.org/strategies/panel/clts/index.html.
18. Davis, *Starting a Community Land Trust*.
19. See https://groundedsolutions.org/.

Affordable Housing

Making Housing Happen: Faith-Based Affordable Housing Models

Edited by the previously mentioned Jill Shook, this book[20] is an indispensable guide framing affordable housing as a justice issue. Includes many case studies to whet the appetite!

Communities of Faith and Affordable Housing

An online toolkit[21] provided under the auspices of the Congress for the New Urbanism. Includes a number of case studies and guidance for churches with land, parking lots, time, or money to contribute towards affordable housing in their community.

Focused Community Strategies (FCS) and the Lupton Center

FCS[22] has worked in South Atlanta for decades, with an emphasis on mixed-income affordable-housing development. They provide a good example of holistic, community-driven affordable-housing efforts. The affiliated Lupton Center[23] provides training in what they call Holistic Neighborhood Development.

Social Ownership of Housing

A broad-based, academically oriented view of affordable housing, including a discussion of a variety of ownership types such as public, nonprofit rental, mutual housing associations, cooperatives, and community land trusts. Written by University of Massachusetts Boston professor Michael E. Stone, available free of charge from the author's academic website.[24]

---

20. Shook, *Making Housing Happen*.
21. See https://www.center4eleadership.org/cnu-faith-housing.
22. See https://www.fcsministries.org/mixedincomehousing.
23. See https://www.luptoncenter.org/.
24. Stone, "Social Ownership."

11

Anchor Institutions

Overview

ANCHOR INSTITUTIONS ARE LARGE, community-rooted organizations such as hospitals, universities, and museums. The mission and success of anchor institutions ("anchors") is intimately tied to the local environment, unlike most for-profit corporations that can move freely in pursuit of higher profits. Although anchors are often incorporated into TED plans, our focus in this chapter is on leveraging anchors to advance the CED goal of equitable economic development. To be considered an anchor for CED purposes, the organization must have a relatively stable budget driven by sizeable employment, with substantial and consistent operating costs. In many cases, large hospitals, particularly nonprofit and university-affiliated hospitals, are the most obvious anchors and form the basis for many of the better-known case studies. Although hospitals need not be the sole focus of an anchor strategy, they are particularly attractive because literally every metropolitan area in the US has at least one major hospital.[1]

As a CED strategy, anchors can drive huge demand for a wide variety of locally sourced products and services, thereby strengthening the local economy and rooting the capital in the community. Although many hospitals abandoned local purchasing strategies in the 1970s in the pursuit of cost savings, there has fortunately been a resurgence of localized procurement

1. Anchor-driven strategies are most relevant in larger or even medium-sized metropolitan areas; many rural areas and small towns lack not only major hospitals, but other candidates for anchors as well.

strategies in the industry. In addition to strengthening the local economy, hospitals and other anchors can realize lower costs, reduce their carbon footprint, and increase resilience by reducing reliance on global supply chains for critical product supplies. Anchors also need a wide variety of localized services such as landscaping, laundering, catering, building management, janitorial, and information technology. Awarding service contracts to locally owned businesses, especially women- and minority-owned, can have a tremendous impact on local economies by strengthening local business networks in an equitable, inclusive manner. Even relatively small shifts in expenditures can result in large influxes of capital for a community. For example, the University of Pennsylvania redirected $80 million back into the local economy by moving just 10 percent of its expenditures to local sources.[2] The numbers can get even bigger: Philadelphia Anchors for Growth & Equity has a goal of localizing $500 million in purchasing from thirteen area hospitals and universities in the coming years.[3]

Centered on the economic procurement engine of the anchor, local businesses can be further strengthened by forming a network of mutually supporting organizations that buy and sell from each other, keeping even more capital circulating in the community. In its strongest form, these networks include community and worker-owned cooperatives to create a truly community-rooted economy (see chapter 6). The original inspiration for this approach is found in the Basque city of Mondragon, Spain, made famous in the United States through the work of the Evergreen Cooperative in Cleveland, Ohio, leading many to name anchor-driven strategies as the "The Cleveland Model."

Getting Started

In many communities, anchors are already active in a variety of community and economic development activities. The quickest way to advance an anchor-based CED strategy is to identify these community-engaged anchors, identify any major new expansion efforts on the horizon, and review their procurement strategy for goods and services. As mentioned above, because anchors are attractive for TED, their economic impact on communities does not necessarily directly benefit vulnerable or marginalized populations. Accountable development (chapter 12), particularly community

2. Burke and Weekes, "UWI Mona Campus," 16.
3. Mastrull, *Philadelphia Launches Push.*

benefits agreements (CBAs), should be pursued to guide anchor development projects, many of which receive substantial public funding. CBAs or similar types of agreements have been generated in many communities to ensure anchors pursue equitable hiring practices, invest in affordable and worker housing, support local business creation, and fund a whole host of community-building activities. Such efforts are key to ensuring that anchor operations and new developments, especially those by mission-driven anchors, explicitly incorporate benefits for low-income and other marginalized communities.

Aside from major expansion efforts, community-engaged anchors can be a vast source of untapped potential for CED by recasting their procurement policies and practices. The first step is to work with the anchor to determine the current level of local sourcing for institutional goods and services. Unfortunately, it is typical to find very low levels of local sourcing, with traditional procurement practices focused on economies of scale and risk reduction rather than local economic development. Shifting procurement practices can start with very targeted approaches, for example, transferring food and beverage purchasing from large national suppliers to local vendors, or requiring those national suppliers to purchase from local vendors. Procurement strategies can also be targeted to help bolster particularly under-represented populations or communities within a metropolitan area. For example, many anchors commit to targets for minority and women-owned contracts with respect to large development efforts. This same principle can be applied to procurement practices, with commitments to award service contracts in areas such as painting, window washing, and building maintenance, to businesses in underserved neighborhoods or communities. Even though many mission-driven anchors have high-level commitments to support the local community, CED practitioners must ensure that these well-meaning commitments that sound good in the boardroom actually translate into practices that truly benefit those populations and communities most in need.

In order to get anchors to shift procurement towards local sources, the local business ecosystem must be able to meet the needs of large scale institutions, including rigorous contracting and delivery standards. Here we can see the power of an interconnected CED strategy, with an anchor strategy coupled to business incubation (chapter 5), self-employment/microbusiness support (chapter 3), makerspace development (chapter 4), workforce development to support hiring of marginalized populations (chapter 7),

JESUS ON MAIN STREET

and technical assistance services to help local businesses qualify as vendors with large anchors. This approach is even more attractive when anchors are tapped as potential funders for these related CED efforts, especially if they are packaged as part of an overall strategy for those anchors to support the local economy through localized procurement.

Such efforts are most likely to succeed if they start with a focus on a particular cluster of services, for example locally sourced food and beverage. CED can also help small businesses, even microbusinesses, work together when the local community may not have a single business with enough scale to meet the demands of the anchor. Such a strategy could apply in areas as diverse as cleaning services, garment/uniform production, landscaping, building maintenance, and food service. In its fullest form, such endeavors could result in the creation of worker-cooperatives, such as the Evergreen Cooperative Laundry.[4] Cooperatives are discussed in more detail in chapter 6.

The Role of Churches

Churches and faith communities in general can play a role in anchor-based CED in much the same way as with accountable development (chapter 12). That is, churches can call attention to economic injustice and organize to call anchors to live up to their missions. As Jesus followers, we have a special calling to pursue those forgotten and marginalized segments of our communities, and in the case of anchor-based CED, to help these community members participate in the economic bounty that often proceeds from these anchors.

This author is not aware of cases where churches are the primary instigators of an anchor-based CED strategy. However, as mentioned above, because of the interconnected nature of CED, an anchor strategy is likely to require incorporating several CED activities that could directly benefit from local church support. The following illustration is meant to inspire creativity and innovation to design church-based CED anchor strategies that leverage efforts in which churches may already be active.

Some churches have programs to support incoming refugees and other immigrants within the community. While churches often provide crucial material, financial, and social startup assistance, immigrants often struggle to find living-wage work in the United States, even with impressive

4. See http://www.evgoh.com/feature/evergreen-cooperative-laundry/.

skills and credentials from their home country. Makerspace (chapter 4) and business-incubation services (chapter 5) could provide space and support to turn immigrant skills, for example sewing or tailoring, into a business. If a cluster of immigrants has this particular skill or can develop it, they could receive help in forming a worker-cooperative (chapter 6) or a conventional business to provide uniform services to an anchor. Whereas it would likely be impossible for these skilled individuals to provide services directly to anchors, a competitive, qualified business can be formed collectively with the support of local churches and other CED specialists. This same concept could apply to other areas such as food service, landscaping, painting, laundering, and more. The key is to take an existing church focus area (immigrant and refugee support in this example) and develop a CED strategy around this.

Further, many churches have members with specialized skills and connections that could help this strategy succeed. For example, attorneys could provide pro-bono support for business incorporation, licensing, and registration, as well as help with the development and negotiation of service contracts with anchors. Accountants could aid in establishing financial systems for the business, and those with management experience can provide leadership mentoring. Wealthy church members could provide needed startup capital in the form of grants, low-interest loans, or equity investment. In all cases, however, the leadership and decision-making structures of the newly formed business ventures *must* be provided by the immigrant community, with the supporting church providing advisory services. The result is a sustainable business to bless the immigrants and the surrounding community, with church members being blessed as well when they see their God-given "secular" talents being used to bless the community.

Challenges

What if your community has no obvious anchors? Certainly, smaller metropolitan areas, rural communities, as well as regions suffering from long-term economic decline, may lack anchors with the characteristics laid out above. In these cases, other candidates for localized procurement strategies may be considered—for example, large- or medium-sized businesses in these communities. Even smaller businesses have supply chains for needed goods and services. Chapter 6 includes a discussion of how business networks can be formed to keep as much capital in the community as possible, with businesses of all sizes buying and selling from each other.

Because anchor-institution strategies have become trendy in economic development circles, TED-driven anchor strategies don't necessarily align with the CED goals of equitable economic development. Particularly in cities with strong economic-development departments, CED practitioners may find resistance to giving them access to the anchors for fear of upsetting TED plans. This is similar to challenges faced with accountable development and CBAs discussed in chapter 12, calling churches to potentially play a role in community organizing to open up direct channels between the community and its anchor institutions.

Finally, even strongly mission-driven anchors must be held accountable for providing equitable benefits. In many cases, anchors are prestigious institutions with storied histories and financial support from the upper echelons of society, particularly in the case of museums and other cultural institutions. Maintaining social and financial ties to local elites may keep executives at anchors from fully embracing CED calls for equitable economic impacts, perhaps because it also shines a light on the business practices of anchor supporters. Thus, all CED anchor strategies must incorporate provisions for regular, transparent reporting and processes to enforce agreed-upon goals and objectives.

Case Study: Evergreen Cooperative

Since much has been written about the Cleveland Model and the Evergreen Cooperative, a very brief summary will be provided here with links below for further reading. The genesis for this initiative was a major expansion project of University Hospitals, a large nonprofit medical center in Cleveland, Ohio. A commitment to equitable economic impacts was core to the program, with many CBA-type agreements incorporated into the work. The Cleveland Foundation provided a sizeable grant to the Democracy Collaborative to envision and start worker-cooperatives to serve the many institutions in and around the University Hospitals complex. Evergreen Cooperative Laundry, the first such business, was launched in 2008, joined by several other cooperatives subsequently created to provide energy-efficiency upgrades and food production. Evergreen Cooperatives continues to this day as a thriving organization committed to launching and supporting employee-owned business ventures.[5]

Further Reading and Exploration

Democracy Collaborative Anchor Institutions Overview

A significant repository of online information[6] on anchor institutions with research reports, videos, and publications.

Journal on Anchor Institutions and Communities

A freely available, quasi-academic journal[7] that provides a wealth of anchor case studies.

Central Corridor Anchor Partnership

An initiative[8] providing an example of how a number of smaller anchors can work together to provide a sizeable impact, with estimates of over $300 million in opportunity from shifting procurement from out-of-state vendors to local vendors.

Leadership in Equitable Anchor Procurement (LEAP)

LEAP[9] is a program focused on bringing minority-owned businesses together with anchors and local governments to create localized procurement opportunities. Support and training is available to bring the LEAP model to communities across the nation.

---

5. For a complete case study, see Wang, *Cleveland Evergreen Cooperatives*. See the Cleveland Model page at community-wealth.org for a variety of articles and videos.

6. See https://community-wealth.org/strategies/panel/anchors/index.html.

7. See Anchor Institutions Task Force, *Journal on Anchor Institutions and Communities*, vols. 1–2.

8. See https://www.centralcorridoranchorpartnership.org/.

9. See https://interise.org/programs/leap/.

12

Accountable Development

Overview

As DISCUSSED IN CHAPTER 1, many TED efforts contribute to inequality by directly benefitting those with political and economic power, with limited benefits towards marginalized communities. Even worse, not only do these communities fail to receive benefits, they are often *negatively impacted* through physical and cultural displacement, escalating housing costs, and a proliferation of low-wage work with long commutes. The premise of accountable development is that large-scale development should provide significant benefits to marginalized communities, including poorer residents and workers. Called by various other names such as the New Accountable Development Movement (NADM),[1] Economic Inclusion,[2] and Responsible Development,[3] accountable development is unfortunately often left out of CED plans. Granted, accountable development seeks to leverage and guide large-scale developments that are well beyond most CED efforts, for example market-rate housing developments, sports arenas, large retail/commercial centers, and expanded corporate facilities. However, while developments such as these are often met with enthusiasm by local government officials and business leaders, ensuring that benefits accrue to vulnerable communities requires significant organizing, planning, and negotiating at the community level—a perfect job for CED!

1. Parks and Warren, *Politics and Practice of Economic Justice.*
2. Schachtel, *East Baltimore Revitalization Initiative.*
3. See *Building a Better Bay Area.*

A range of tools are available to ensure that major economic development activities benefit vulnerable populations. Accountable development tools include community benefits agreements (CBAs), living-wage movements and ordinances, first-source hiring agreements, superstore ordinances, inclusionary zoning, and more. CBAs, the focus of this chapter, are project-based agreements between the community and a developer[4] in response to specific, proposed development. The chapter will include a brief discussion of the other elements that comprise accountable development, but since these typically first require work at the policy and legislative level, the treatment will only be cursory.

Getting Started

While the contents of a CBA are critical, the processes created and followed may be even more important. Esteemed planner, architect, and social-justice advocate Dr. Carl Anthony suggests that "instead of seeing community benefit campaigns as only a means to get a certain kind of development, we need to start thinking about the development process as a means for helping to build stronger and more engaged communities . . . [they are] just as much about engagement and empowerment of communities as they are about the specific outcomes from development projects."[5]

In addition to generating an opportunity for community building, experience shows that strong community organizing is a necessary input to a successful CBA process. Without effective organizing, the "community" represented in a CBA will be incomplete at best, potentially reinforcing existing levels of inequality and marginalization and even fracturing a community. If a community already has a working community organizing process with a lead organization or individual, the CBA process will demand their best work. Otherwise, communities should consider bringing in a seasoned community organizer to not only shepherd the CBA process, but to develop organizing capabilities within the community itself. Faith in Action[6] is a national organizing network focused on building strong, faith-rooted organizing efforts throughout the country with training and

---

4. CBAs are distinct from agreements between the developer and the local government ("development agreements") and agreements between communities and government ("cooperation agreements").

5. See *Building a Better Bay Area*, 2.

6. See www.faithinaction.org.

support available to start an effort in your community. More resources are listed at the end of this chapter.

Further, experience has shown that community-labor coalitions are most successful in creating and implementing CBAs. Communities located in cities with a strong labor presence should seek to develop partnerships with these organizations, as prescribed by Partnership for Working Families.[7]

Contents of a CBA

The contents of a CBA are highly dependent on the nature of the development project, how that project may affect the community, and unmet needs in the community. For example, if an influx of new employees to the area is expected, a CBA can require that a percentage of the development budget be allocated for affordable housing to help offset increased demand for existing housing. In cases where new high-paying jobs are promised, incorporating funding for job training and workforce development into a CBA can address the mismatch between requirements for these new jobs and qualifications of existing residents. Justifications for new development often include the indirect creation of new jobs in retail and service industries, without acknowledging that most of these are low-wage jobs with minimal benefits. Recognizing that many community members will continue to work in these low-wage jobs, CBAs can require funding for subsidized affordable day care, sick pay funding, and other programs benefiting low-income individuals and families in the community. CBAs also may incorporate "good jobs" provisions (chapter 9) to ensure that all development-related positions, as well as positions created by business tenants of the development, pay a locally appropriate living wage and meet other "good jobs" criteria.

First-source hiring agreements can be incorporated into CBAs, requiring that the employers associated with the development draw on local community training centers and other designated "first sources" for local job applicants. Targeted hiring provisions can mandate that developers hire local workers and firms, including targets for minority/women-owned businesses. In cases of large retail center development ("superstores"), CBAs can require the developer to pay for an independent Economic Impact Analysis (EIA) to determine impacts on traffic, land use, social structures,

7. See www.communitybenefits.org for more details and examples.

and local economic health. CBAs can bolster the prospects for local small businesses who often struggle competing against such superstores, designating funding for small business support and investment as identified in the EIA. Finally, CBAs often help fund general community improvements such as traffic-congestion mitigation, bike lanes, green space/park development, and even community-center facility development.

Monitoring and Enforcement

The Achilles heel of many well-intentioned CBA efforts is a lack of monitoring and enforcement for the provisions of the CBA. For example, if the developer agrees to hire a hundred local residents at an agreed-upon living wage, or agrees to provide a specific amount of funding for affordable housing, how will progress against these goals be tracked and what happens if these goals are not met? To begin, the language of CBAs must provide clear and legally enforceable conditions, with specific developer goals, timelines for compliance, reporting requirements, and consequences of noncompliance clearly specified. The simple act of documenting these items in a CBA is a vast improvement over typical TED agreements in which local and state governments provide large tax incentives to corporations and developers in exchange for vague goals with no consequences for noncompliance. Indeed, elected officials are typically leery of drawing attention to development that fails to live up to its promise, focusing instead on the ribbon-cutting photo-ops when the promises are still fresh but unproven. Transparent reporting requirements in CBAs can ensure that promises are not buried in yesterday's headlines.

As is the case with accountable development in general, successful CBA monitoring and enforcement is predicated on strong and effective organizing. Although the CBA agreement as a legal instrument is important, CBAs are primarily political in nature, i.e., they require developing coalitions spanning government, labor, community, and business in order to gain support for the CBA and the enforcement process. Community-driven oversight for the CBA's implementation can be established on a foundation of strong organizing, incorporating a transparent process to monitor the developer's commitments and report on compliance or noncompliance. For example, a typical non-compliance clause is to require developers to repay tax incentives if certain goals are not met. These so-called "claw back" provisions provide real teeth to monitoring and enforcement efforts, but obviously require working closely with the appropriate governmental entities to not only gain support for the inclusion of the claw back provision in the CBA, but to also agree to include such a provision in their own agreements with developers and demand repayment in the case of non-compliance.

The Role of Churches

There is a strong tradition in the United States of faith communities playing crucial roles in building coalitions around a variety of social-justice issues, including economic justice. Organizations may be national in scope, such as the previously mentioned Faith in Action; regionally focused, such as Clergy and Laity United for Economic Justice (CLUE);[8] or city-specific, such as Nashville Organized for Action and Hope.[9] Churches interested in supporting accountable development must develop and maintain a strong commitment to justice in their teaching and preaching, as well as provide members with opportunities and connections to get involved. Clergy and laity who are energized by a faith-rooted commitment to justice can be valuable partners in the hard work of community organizing that is vital to successful accountable development efforts. The faith community can be instrumental in seeking out the one sheep that got away from the ninety-nine, ensuring that forgotten or marginalized voices within the community are brought into organizing efforts, and guarding against CBAs that may privilege certain community members or constituencies while ignoring others.

Challenges

Unsuccessful CBA efforts typically stem from bad process, with some community stakeholders feeling left out, or local governments managing the entire process with well-controlled outreach sessions to polish agreements that are largely already complete. Local officials may balk at allowing a "troublesome" community group to impede negotiations for a major development, worried that their city may be perceived as anti-business. However, it is critical that communities negotiate *directly* with the developer, something

8. See https://www.cluejustice.org/.
9. See https://www.noahtn.org/.

that many local governments, especially those with strong economic development departments, are loath to allow even though they lack the legal or moral standing to prohibit it. Overcoming such a barrier may require well-orchestrated protest and organizing activities, drawing attention to overzealous politicians giving away large amounts of money for ill-defined and unenforceable promises. It will also require clear communication and engagement with a variety of community and labor groups, enlisting them to challenge local officials to support strong, enforceable CBAs.

Another challenge is that successful CBA efforts require a community to establish its capacity for organizing well before time-critical development proposals are announced. This likely will require cutting your organizing teeth on less controversial and less complex projects such as community gardens, street lighting, park improvements, beautification efforts, and a whole host of other traditional community development and locality development (chapter 10) activities.

Build Relationship for when you need them

Power you have to do

Case Study: Nashville Organized for Action and Hope

Nashville Organized for Action and Hope[10] (NOAH) is a multi-racial, interdenominational, faith-led coalition working to give voice to marginalized people in areas including affordable housing, economic equity, and education. By incorporating congregations, community organizations, and labor unions into its coalition, NOAH has successfully organized efforts to influence the passage of local hiring mandates for Metro projects and the development of workforce-readiness programs. Perhaps its biggest success to date is the completion of a CBA to ensure that the development of a stadium for Nashville's Major League Soccer team provided a wide range of benefits to the city's diverse population. Taking on such a task required additional coalition building, resulting in NOAH helping to create the Stand Up Nashville (SUN) Coalition[11] to organize for accountable development. SUN, comprising a wide variety of community organizations and labor unions, negotiated a CBA[12] delivering a wide range of benefits including:

- 20 percent of the housing units built at the development site to be affordable and workforce housing

10. See https://www.noahtn.org/.
11. See http://standupnashville.org/.
12. A complete copy of the CBA is available on the Stand Up Nashville wesbite.

- Minimum $15.50/hour for all stadium workers with a targeted hiring program for individuals with employment barriers

- 4,000 square feet of development site dedicated for a childcare facility with a sliding fee schedule

- Additional 4,000 square feet dedicated to micro-spaces for artisans and local small businesses at reduced rental rates

- Construction/contracting job training and hiring practices for individuals with barriers to employment, with special consideration for minority contractors

- Establishment of a committee with community representation to monitor and report on compliance

Perhaps most striking about the work of NOAH is the extent of its coalition building. With nearly seventy dues-paying member congregations, NOAH has been very successful in not only building a broad coalition of faith communities, but in developing an aggressive justice-oriented platform. NOAH has presented its platform to literally thousands of community members and engaged with Nashville mayoral candidates to ensure that NOAH platform issues were addressed in city government. However, when presented with the challenge of guiding the development of a new soccer stadium, NOAH realized that an even broader coalition was required, resulting in the formation of the SUN coalition comprised of eight community and labor organizations. Strong coalition building and inclusive community organizing were key to success for the powerful and effective CBA described above.

Further Reading and Exploration

Building a Better Bay Area

This report[13] provides an excellent overview of Responsible Development and CBAs. Includes fifteen case studies highlighting a wide range of contexts for pursuing CBAs and specific terms built into successfully negotiated agreements.

13. See *Building a Better Bay Area.*

Northwest Bronx Community and Clergy Coalition (NWBCCC)

NWBCCC[14] is a locally rooted, faith-led organization fighting for racial and economic justice through a variety of community organizing efforts. Particularly noteworthy is their involvement in shutting down the proposed redevelopment of a vacant property into a low-wage mall, followed by the successful negotiation of a CBA through the Kingsbridge Armory Redevelopment Alliance.

Partnership for Working Families

This national network[15] of regional affiliates is on the forefront of work in accountable development. Their "Community Benefits 101" site provides an online planning tool and "CBAs Currently in Effect" with the actual text of the agreements included.[16]

Good Jobs First

A national clearinghouse[17] of information on accountable development, including a beginner's guide, researcher's guide, and model legislation.

Faith-Rooted Organizing

This vital book[18] by Alexia Salvatierra and Peter Heltzel provides a model for faith-based organizing. The authors build on and extend traditional community-organizing principles and practices to incorporate God's vision for shalom and the good news of the gospel.

14. See https://www.northwestbronx.org/economic-development.
15. See https://www.forworkingfamilies.org/.
16. See https://www.forworkingfamilies.org/page/cba-101.
17. See https://www.goodjobsfirst.org/accountable-development.
18. Salvatierra and Heltzel, *Faith-Rooted Organizing*.

Faith in Action

As mentioned previously, this national organization[19] with numerous local affiliates provides a variety of resources and training for faith-based organizing efforts. Faith in Action envisions a "Moral Economy" with a strong history of actions to bring about accountable development across the country. For cities without a local affiliate, they provide help to start local faith-based organizing efforts.

Midwest Academy

A national training institute[20] providing courses and consulting services in community organizing.

---

19. See https://www.faithinaction.org/issue-campaign/moral-economy/.
20. See https://www.midwestacademy.com/.

PART 3

*Community
Economic Development Process*

13

Assessment and Implementation Process

Overview

UNDERSTANDING THE TOOLKIT OF possible CED strategies is just the first step in walking with Jesus down Main Street. Here in Part 3, we focus our attention on turning dreams and ideas into real impact. Before delving into our recommended assessment and implementation process, we acknowledge that the structure provided in this chapter may appeal to some but feel restrictive and stifling to others. If Jesus is inviting you to join him on Main Street, you *must* follow him, with or without the structure of strategic planning. We acknowledge that impossible things are possible with God, and that if God is calling you, your church *will* have tremendous impacts on your local economy. We offer the process laid out in this chapter as a way to expand possibilities and help turn ideas into reality, not as a mechanism to justify saying no to audacious visions for community thriving.

Most strategic-planning processes follow the same basic structure: (1) establish mission and vision, (2) assessment, (3) strategy formulation, (4) implementation, and (5) evaluation and adaptation. This chapter assumes you already have some experience with strategic planning in other contexts, for example, in guiding a community nonprofit or developing an overall strategy for your church. Our focus here will be a general overview of the CED process within this basic five-step framework, with some special adaptations and considerations for church-based CED. The majority of this chapter will focus on assessment (step 2) along with a discussion of establishing a strategic approach (step 3). A number of worksheet templates are provided at the end of the chapter to guide your efforts in planning and implementing CED.[1]

Step 1: Establish Mission and Vision

As mentioned in the introduction to this book, establishing your church's mission, vision, and values around justice and a holistic definition of the gospel is a foundational step for any church considering CED. For example, could you explain to a first-time visitor how your church's workforce-development program or makerspace facility flows from and supports your church's mission, vision, and values? Why does it make sense to pour time and money into these endeavors as opposed to other more traditional church activities? While it is beyond the scope of this book to discuss processes to craft church mission, vision, and values, you may consider works on social justice[2] and missional theology[3] along with suggestions from the introduction[4] to guide your thinking.

CED assumes a place-based focus, normally at the level of a neighborhood or a specific section of a city. In other words, what is the "community" for your CED work? If you church already has a well-defined sense of parish,[5] then this is where your CED work will naturally focus. For churches without a strong sense of place, such as commuter churches, or those located in affluent bedroom communities, part of your mission-crafting work should include identifying specific places to focus your mission and ministry. Strategies and implications for CED in such scenarios will be covered in more depth in chapter 14 below.

Assuming a holistic, place-based mission rooted in God's justice, most of the CED strategies and activities discussed in this book will be within the scope of consideration for your church. However, the way in which your church approaches CED can look very different depending on your church

1. Worksheets are available online at https://jesusonmainstreet.com/worksheets.

2. See for example Sider, *Good News and Good Works* and Suttle, *An Evangelical Social Gospel?*

3. See for example, Frost and Hirsch, *Shaping of Things To Come*. Also see https://www.goodreads.com/shelf/show/missional-theology for an extensive reading list, including guidance on leading your church towards a missional theology.

4. Wytsma, *Pursuing Justice*; Stearns, *Hole in Our Gospel*.

5. See Sparks et al., *New Parish*.

and community context. This leads naturally to the second, and in our opinion, the most important step in the CED planning process: assessment.

Step 2: Assessment

Leaders who are inclined to fast action and feel they already understand their community may question the need for this step. However, a robust and deliberate assessment process is critical in order to decenter the church and ensure a collaborative approach to CED. A "decentered" posture may be particularly difficult for churches and leaders who are used to being in the driver's seat and may worry about diluting the church's impact or compromising the church's values. The reality is that supporting collaborative CED efforts will *expand* your church's impact, with multiplicative rather than additive impact.[6] Also, rooting your church's mission, vision, and values as described above will provide ongoing guidance and protection against compromise that may arise in a heavily collaborative process.

There are four elements that comprise a thorough CED assessment: (1) your community's CED ecosystem; (2) your church's fit within that CED ecosystem; (3) community demographic, income, employment trends; and (4) your community's broader assets and needs. Although we present them in linear fashion, the first three assessment elements can proceed roughly simultaneously. The final element of our assessment provides a useful wrapper for the entire assessment process, using a modified version of a tool that will already be familiar to many readers: the asset map from Asset Based Community Development (ABCD).[7] If you have already developed an asset map of your community as part of an ABCD effort, you may find some elements will transfer directly, with many new assets identified as we apply our CED lens.

Another tool, the traditional metropolitan-level economic study, is useful, but not sufficient for CED planning. TED professionals typically commission such studies to examine region-wide demographic and employment trends, business infrastructure, industry clusters, economic multipliers, and more. Such studies are available freely from local government economic-development agencies in most metropolitan areas, and we recommend you read them carefully and thoroughly. You should also examine your city's economic-development strategic plans to understand

6. See the Introduction for more on CED as a multiplicative versus additive strategy.

7. See https://resources.depaul.edu/abcd-institute.

the focus of city- or region-wide economic development. While CED can be informed by these TED studies and reports, more often than not their primary value is to highlight TED's shortcomings in reaching your community and its most vulnerable members. These documents can also provide context and insight into the types of TED activities that are going on in your city, highlighting appropriate targets for accountable development interventions (chapter 12).

Your Community's CED Ecosystem

The first phase of assessment focuses on your community's CED assets and activities. Start by determining which CED programs are available in your community using the CED toolkit from part 2 of this book as a guide for the types of programs to look for. Such programs may be provided by community development corporations, nonprofits, churches, or local government. For existing programs, you should determine the targeted populations and geographic scope and ask if they are effectively reaching your community, particularly its most vulnerable members. Interviews with the leaders of these programs, along with organizational annual reports and third party evaluations, can be useful when available. A simple worksheet, entitled "CED Ecosystem Program Assessment Worksheet 1," is provided below to guide you in this phase of the assessment.

In addition to a program-centric view, your CED ecosystem assessment should create an inventory or asset map of individuals and organizations involved in CED. Here it is useful to distinguish individuals by the four types of CED roles discussed in chapter 2: consultant, enabler, organizer, participant. The organizations should be categorized by their general approach or method, also covered in chapter 2: development, community organizing, policy and planning interventions. In addition to providing a useful set of potential CED allies, such an inventory can help identify holes in your community's CED ecosystem and determine its overall cohesiveness. This assessment will also help you determine if a community economic development organization is already providing overall guidance to foster collaboration or if everybody is working in relative isolation. See the worksheet "CED Individuals and Organizations Assessment Worksheet 2" for a template to guide this phase of the assessment.

Your Church's Fit within the Ecosystem

Building on the CED ecosystem assessment above, the next phase of assessment is to determine how your church can best fit within and support this ecosystem to maximize community thriving. Note that at this point, the goal is not to identify specific CED programs or strategies to pursue; that will require an assessment of your community's overall assets and needs, which is still to come. Rather, your focus here should be to identify a candidate list of programs and/or target populations that may be weak or missing from the current CED ecosystem, as revealed in Worksheet 1. If you have specific expertise, or can draw on that expertise from church members, you can prioritize several of these candidate programs for more deliberate consideration later. See "Church Fit within CED Ecosystem Worksheet 3" for a template to guide you.

This phase of the assessment also looks at the roles you and your members will personally fulfill in the CED ecosystem, as well as your church's organizational approach to CED. Therefore, Worksheet 3 includes guidance to match the skills, passions, and capacities of your church with the needs in your community's CED ecosystem. Assuming that you personally will be leading your church's CED efforts, will you fit into the CED ecosystem as a consultant, enabler, organizer, or participant?[8] Most pastors are likely to be enablers or organizers, drawing on their community connections and relationship-building skills. Considering your CED core team and interested individuals within your church, which of these roles will they fulfill? If individuals have specific finance, legal, or business experience, they could be considered as consultants. In some cases, you or members of your church may be participants, with roles in starting or running a CED program or business/social venture.

From an organizational perspective, will your church approach CED as a developer/program deliverer, community organizer, or as a policy and planning intervener? Worksheet 2 may reveal what type of approach is needed in your community. For example, it is common to find that many existing community organizations focus on development and program-delivery work, indicative of a long-term trend among community nonprofits away from advocacy and organizing.[9] On the other hand, you may find

---

8. See chapter 2 for definitions.

9. This widely reported trend has been linked to funders increasingly looking for "tangible" outcomes associated with development and program-delivery work. Community organizing and policy-advocacy work are also often unattractive to funders because

plenty of organizers and planners, but a need for more organizations to deliver specific programs or reach forgotten segments of the population. If your community already has an economic-development organization dedicated to CED in your community, we recommend you explore partnering with them and filling out the ecosystem by offering missing programs, reaching underserved populations, providing community-organizing support, or advocating for policy changes. If your community is lacking a community economic-development organization, you must determine if starting a separate nonprofit organization to guide the entire collaborative process is warranted and if your church is up for the challenge. In most cases, the answer will be to first gain some experience by launching a CED program and developing connections and credibility within the CED ecosystem. Mihailo Temali's CED handbook provides useful guidance if you decide to start your own economic-development nonprofit.[10]

While some churches can fill multiple roles, we recommend you pick one primary role and look to collaboratively build out the CED ecosystem to fill other roles and approaches as required. The goal for this phase of the assessment is to *start* discerning your church's focus area and type of involvement in CED. Completing this process will require the next phases of assessment, looking at the greater community, with the ultimate decision deferred until step 3 below.

Community Demographic, Income, and Employment Trends

As discussed above, a metropolitan-level economic study can provide good context on overall trends impacting your community. Such reports typically include information on industry sectors that are growing or declining in your area and projected sources of jobs in the coming years. However, even if such a report is available to you, it will likely not have detailed information on your community of interest. The primary questions that will still need to be answered include: (1) how has your community changed over time, (2) how does your community differ from the overall metropolitan region, and (3) how are vulnerable or marginalized groups faring? Fortunately, there are many sources of data that can be easily accessed to

---

of the disruptive nature of such work, leading to changes that are not necessarily aligned with the interests of community elites.

10. See Temali, *Community Economic Development Handbook*, ch. 2.

answer these questions.[11] Below we provide a brief overview of two of the most useful tools.

Social Explorer

Social Explorer[12] provides a visual interface to many data sources covering demographics, economy, crime, health, politics, and more. Although this is a for-fee service, it is cancellable during a seven day free trial period, with no long-term contract commitment.

Social Explorer's map-based view is particularly insightful, showing how key statistics such as household income, percentage racial/ethnic categories, education levels, occupation and employment status, housing status, and much more, vary by census tract level. Because the tool includes historic data, you can also see how these key statistics have changed over time, uncovering trends such as the displacement of low-income residents to far-flung suburbs, or the movement of racial and ethnic minorities through the city over time. While the specific data of interest will vary based on the eventual focus of your CED programs, we recommend you start by viewing how racial and ethnic percentages, income levels, and unemployment rates have changed spatially in your community during the last twenty years.

Census Reporter

Census Reporter[13] provides an extremely simple but powerful interface to get a snapshot of your community of interest using standard geographic boundaries including census block groups, census tracts, or school districts. It provides key statistics such as age, race/ethnicity, income and poverty levels, owner/renter status, and more. The report also compares each of these statistics to the surrounding county and state.

---

11. For a complete overview of relevant data sources with sample reports, see Kresta, "Database Summaries."

12. See https://www.socialexplorer.com.

13. See https://censusreporter.org/locate/.

Community Assets and Needs

This final assessment element will help answer the question of exactly what type of CED program you should pursue based on existing community assets and economic development needs. As mentioned above, the primary tool we use to wrap up our assessment is a modified version of the ABCD asset map. Current ABCD practice identifies a total of six types of community assets: (1) residents, (2) associations, (3) institutions, (4) physical space, (5) economic/exchange, and (6) culture/stories/history.[14] Before embarking on this final stage of assessment, we recommend you reach out to other community groups, particularly local community development corporations (CDCs), to determined if they have developed an ABCD asset map that you can use as your starting point. While a complete ABCD asset map[15] would be a useful resource to leverage at this stage, it is not required. Instead, we provide focused guidance below and in the "CED Asset Map Worksheet 4."

Although ABCD asset mapping typically starts with individuals, we recommend starting CED asset mapping with a preliminary assessment of associations and institutions. While these organizations are important because of the direct role they may play in CED, they can also help you to identify individuals/residents to include in your asset mapping. The opposite is also true: discussions with individuals can uncover additional associations and institutions. In other words, the various asset categories should be used to inform each other and not be treated as silos.

Associations

Local associations are residents organized around some commonality such as where they live, cultural/ethnic values, faith, business interests, social causes, as well as local chapters of larger organizations. Local resident

14. The last asset category, culture/story/history, is important for general community development efforts and should be well understood by all churches, even those not pursuing CED. The Community Demographic, Income, Employment Trends analysis described above provides a data-driven view into your neighborhood's history. Such analysis must be bolstered by "walking around and talking" research. A full treatment of this asset category, however, is beyond the scope of this book.

15. It is beyond the scope of this book to provide an overview of ABCD. See https://resources.depaul.edu/abcd-institute for books and other training resources. For application of ABCD in a faith-community setting, see Altman and Rans, *Asset-Based Strategies for Faith Communities*.

associations are critical but often overlooked assets of a community, and they typically play a central role in community-development activities. While they may be formal, as in the case of official neighborhood or home-owner associations, they can also be very informal. For CED purposes, associations can help to connect CED programs to underserved populations, connect you to potential entrepreneurs, and provide access to groups of business owners. While all associations may be of interest, we recommend you focus your initial assessment on (1) those oriented around minorities, low-income populations, special-needs, or other groups you are interested in reaching; (2) those with a specific business focus such as business associations, networking groups, unions/worker groups; (3) hobby, craft, or creative groups that may be interested in microbusinesses; and (4) neighborhood improvement and advocacy groups that can be valuable allies (or opponents) to CED efforts in your community.[16]

Institutions

Institutions are formal organizations such as nonprofits, schools, businesses, hospitals, foundations, churches, and government agencies.[17] As crucial CED assets, institutions are valuable employers, drive demand for local purchasing, provide political connections and credibility, and may be sources of funding for CED programs. Anchor institutions (see chapter 11) should be a central feature of your institutional mapping because they can be particularly valuable for CED efforts. Depending on the geographic size of your community, a full inventory of businesses may be overwhelming and not particularly useful.[18] Focus instead on larger employers, women- and minority-owned businesses, locally owned businesses, and developers who have been active within your community. Concentrating on specific industries such as food service or small manufacturing can be another useful way to focus the mapping of businesses for your specific CED interests.

---

16. For a complete review of association mapping, see Turner et al., *Guide to Mapping and Mobilizing the Associations in Local Neighborhoods.*

17. You may have already identified many institutions in Worksheet 2 when you assessed your community's CED ecosystem; copy them here to ensure all community assets are represented in Worksheet 4.

18. For a detailed description of business asset mapping, see Kretzmann and McKnight, *Guide to Mapping Local Business Assets and Mobilizing Local Business Capacities.*

Residents

When asset mapping associations and institutions above, you will naturally be interacting with individuals interested and involved in your community. This phase of assessment focuses specifically on residents, finding potential contributors to CED efforts either because of specific skills they may possess or connections with associations and institutions. Resident mapping can also identify individuals or groups of individuals who may benefit from CED programs such as workforce development or microbusiness support. While a full-coverage resident survey,[19] as a component of an ABCD program, can be useful and should be pursued if budget and time allow, you can focus your efforts by thinking about groups of residents, as provided in Worksheet 4. Examples of groups include minorities or immigrants, members of associations, and online neighborhood groups on a variety of platforms. Fellow faith leaders and attendees of your own church are another group to consider, but be careful to focus only on those who actually live in the community and ensure that your assessment is representative of *all* neighborhood residents, not only those involved in your faith community. Finally, be on the lookout for the unconnected, i.e., those who may not participate in associations, attend church, or otherwise engage with the neighborhood. Walking your neighborhood, hanging out in parks, and simply talking to people can connect you to these residents who may be hidden community assets.

Physical Space

CED views locality and space as an asset to be curated and nurtured for the benefit of all. Traditional ABCD asset mapping incorporates the development of an actual map to catalog the physical space, with block-by-block details on buildings, parks, open spaces, and more. Google Maps has made such mapping much easier than in the past and we encourage supplementing such digital map making with a walking tour, paying particular attention to underutilized buildings and land. Remember to include your own church and other churches in the mapping, noting how these spaces contribute to or detract from the vitality of the surrounding community. Worksheet 4 provides additional elements to include in your physical space

19. For a complete overview of resident asset mapping, see Kretzmann and McKnight, *Guide to Capacity Inventories*.

mapping, including major landmarks/buildings, transportation assets, community hubs where people congregate, as well as economic hubs.

Economic/Exchange

The most obvious components of this last asset category, economic/exchange, will already have been covered above: businesses and anchor institutions, economic hubs, and CED programs and organizations that comprise the CED ecosystem. These assets combine to form the economic backbone for your CED efforts. However, informal economic exchanges such as street vendors and popup shops may uncover a rich system of economic activity just below the surface of the official economy. Such exchanges, as well as informal businesses that advertise via flyers/bulletin boards, social media, and other websites, can be assets from which to build various CED programs, such as microenterprise development (chapter 3) and makerspaces (chapter 4).

But What about Community Needs?

Completing the CED asset mapping as described above and in Worksheet 4 will provide a rich view into how a CED program can be built or strengthened in your community. While the focus is obviously on viewing these elements as community assets, your mapping will also naturally uncover needs or desires for economic change. Having Worksheet 1, with its summary list of potential CED programs and activities, can be useful to spur conversation and inquiries as to which, if any, of the CED programs your interviewees are already involved in, wish they were involved in, or would like to see made available in your community. Worksheet 4 includes space to capture such information to round out your assessment of community assets and needs relevant for CED.

Step 3: Strategy Formulation

Based on the vision/mission foundation from step 1 and the findings from the assessment in step 2, our focus now turns to deciding how you will participate in CED and what programs and activities you will pursue. Working through this decision process can be complex, with incomplete data and perhaps many unknowns. Fortunately, leading a group in discernment with a mixture of prayer, faith, incomplete information, and input from a variety of stakeholders should be familiar ground for many church leaders. It is beyond the scope of this book to layout a specific discernment and group facilitation process, but what we provide below are the questions to answer and the information to consider.

Establish Your Core Team and Advisory Team

While your church's leadership team will provide top-level oversight and support for your CED efforts, you will need two teams exclusively focused on CED. If you haven't already, you should establish a core working team drawn from your church as well as individuals identified in the CED asset mapping exercise as captured in Worksheet 4. While all core team members should have a high-level of commitment to your church's CED efforts and be able to work together, you should also aim for a combination of roles (consultant, enabler, organizer, participant), with special attention to those who can provide expertise from the business sector. We recommend you keep the core team relatively small with no more than five or six people. Your advisory team will provide an opportunity to get broader representation from a wide variety of associations and institutions who can help guide your efforts and provide vital connections to the community. Using Worksheet 4, identify interested individuals from a variety of institutions such as foundations, nonprofits, businesses, anchor institutions, as well as residents from the community, to participate on your advisory team.

Decide Your Church's Role in CED

You should have already begun analyzing options for how your church will participate in CED in Worksheet 3. Now you must decide which primary role you will fulfill: development, community organizing, or policy interventions.[20] While all three are ultimately required in a robust CED ecosystem, we recommend you choose one as your focus. This decision should be based on your CED ecosystem assessment (Worksheet 2) that reveals what roles are already filled in your community, along with further consideration of your church's strengths and calling (Worksheet 3). As discussed

20. See chapter 2 for a refresher on these roles.

in the assessment section above, another consideration is whether to start a separate economic-development nonprofit if your community lacks such an organization. We recommend churches consider this only after getting started with at least one CED program supported by a strong core team and advisory team. For the remainder of this chapter, we assume that your church will take on a development role, which in this context means to play a direct role in delivering programs and services.[21]

Determine Initial Strategic Focus

For our Type A readers, this is the step you've been waiting for! What type of CED program or activity will your church actually do? Again, this is a potentially complex decision, with a large set of tradeoffs, the first of which is to balance community assets and needs with your church's resources/ expertise/interests. Second, your approach can emphasize short-term economic gains through high-impact programs or focus on strengthening the broader CED ecosystem to ensure long-term progress. Third, will your initial focus be driven by opportunistic currents such as an upcoming major development project or funder interest areas, or will you choose to address the highest-need/highest-impact CED efforts based on your assessment? Fourth, which side of the traditional African proverb, "If you want to go fast, go alone, if you want to go far, go together," will you land on? In other words, will you pursue an approach that your church can achieve with limited partnership development, or something that may require significant partnering? Finally, will your approach be geared towards generating the most impact for the most people or will you focus on a specific population that is particularly vulnerable and forgotten by existing programs, even if such a focus limits your top-line dollar impact?

Mihailo Temali suggests a pathway through these tradeoffs by suggesting two conditions for an initial strategy to meet: (1) solves a major community economic problem immediately by taking advantage of existing community assets, and (2) your organization has the resources and capacity in the form of skills and staff time, interested funders and other partners, and synergy with existing programs.[22] Temali also recommends a focus

21. More details on the other two roles is beyond the scope of this book. See Salvatierra and Heltzel, *Faith-Rooted Organizing,* for a good primer on faith-based organizing and policy advocacy.

22. See Temali, *Community Economic Development Handbook,* ch. 2.

on visible economic results as opposed to being fixated on organizational issues, as well as achieving several smaller steps instead of saving up for a big bang sometime in the future. He also notes that CED, particularly in its early days for a community, should look for "symbolic" and "catalytic" projects, i.e., projects that address long-standing, well-known community issues such as a highly visible, dilapidated business center or high unemployment within a particular demographic. Such projects can build momentum and change attitudes in a community, getting others to believe that change is possible and giving them courage to jump in and contribute.

As a final note on choosing an initial strategy, be careful not to confuse projects with a strategy. The items in the CED toolkit from part 2 of this book should not be thought of as isolated projects to complete before moving on to another. Instead, they represent broad strategies to meet CED goals. For example, microenterprise development (chapter 3) comprises a range of projects and activities with the ultimate goal of enabling individuals to reach self-sufficiency through very small businesses. Thus, rather than simply focusing on developing a coaching program for potential microentrepreneurs and tracking the number of graduates through your program (outputs), think about a system of solutions to enable self-sufficiency for your target population (outcomes). Such thinking may suggest a number of interconnected projects or synergistic CED programs: for example, a microbusiness development program, with plans for a makerspace or shared commercial kitchen space that you or a partner will provide. While you should start with a single project with very specific outputs, keep a broader view in mind that incorporates a full solution to reach your hoped-for outcome. This distinction between outputs and outcomes will be elaborated below.

To aid in your decision process, see "CED Initial Strategy Decision Worksheet 5" below. We recommend you work through this worksheet in an extended planning session with your core team, leaving plenty of time for discussion and debate. For each program under consideration (copied over from Worksheet 3), estimate its location along the spectrum for each evaluation criteria. Don't fixate on coming up with an exact answer! The purpose of the worksheet is to help you grapple realistically with each potential program and discuss as a team how you want to approach the various tradeoffs highlighted above. Once your core team has made a decision on which strategy to pursue, we recommend you discuss the reasoning and decision process with several key members of your advisory team to uncover any blind spots before presenting it to the entire advisory team.

Step 4: Implementation

Having formulated your initial strategic approach based on a thorough assessment and solid vision/mission, the next step is to develop an action plan for your initial project and begin implementation. It is beyond the scope of this book to provide an overview of project planning and implementation. Obviously, if you lack this expertise, you'll need to get it on your core team and assign an overall project manager. As depicted in Figure 1, Leigh and Blakely provide a useful three-part structure to consider in the development of a CED action plan with inputs, outputs/outcomes, and an organizational structure. Given our previous discussion on the CED ecosystem, types of CED roles, and the establishment of a core team and advisory team, we will focus here on the other two elements: outputs/outcomes and inputs.

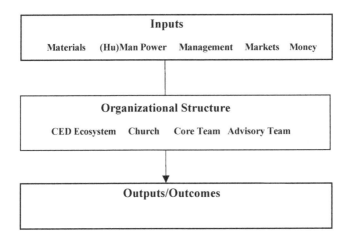

Figure 1: CED action plan components[23]

23. Adapted from Leigh and Blakely, *Planning Local Economic Development*, 221.

Outputs and Outcomes

Starting with the end in mind is always good practice for complex undertakings. Specifying the desired end state enables you to determine the required inputs and organizational structure to realize the outputs and outcomes. Notice that we make the important but often overlooked distinction between *outputs* and *outcomes*. *Outputs* are the activities or services directly delivered by your project, whereas *outcomes* are changes that happen in the community because of your project. CED outcomes will vary depending on your chosen strategy but typically include: (1) employment indicators such as number of new jobs, new jobs by occupation, average wage of new jobs; (2) linkage indicators such as number of local procurement contracts, local residents employed in new jobs, value of locally sourced products and services; and (3) community-improvement indicators such as improved livability scores, community-organizing participation rates, affordable housing units available. Outcomes capture the strategic intent of your project and may be shared across projects or organizations working together towards a common goal over long periods of time.

Outputs on the other hand, are very specific to your organization and project and may change over time as your tactics evolve. For example, if your initial strategy is to establish a business-incubator program, a "curriculum for entrepreneurs" will very likely be a short-term output that must be planned for, implemented, and delivered. Once your program launches, key outputs may include number of local residents who graduate from your program or number of coaches recruited and trained. In both cases, your program is directly responsible for the generation of these outputs. While it is critical to identify and specify these upfront, neither of these outputs should be conflated with the strategic intent of your business incubator program, which is likely some form of "generate local jobs." Unless your program is directly hiring and paying people a wage, the generation of jobs is an *outcome* of your program that occurs in your community. If you train hundreds of entrepreneurs, but none of them actually launches a business and hires employees, you will have successfully delivered on your outputs but failed on outcomes.

We recommend a combination of outputs and outcomes as you create and implement your action plan. In all cases, outputs should have one-year goals established, with longer-term goals at three or five years depending on the program. While outcomes may be short-term ("number of launched businesses within the first year"), more often than not outcomes have longer-term three- and five-year goals that must be tracked over time. For those who wish to implement a more complete planning, implementation, and evaluation process, we recommend developing a logic model.[24] In lieu of the considerable investment required for this approach, however, you may simply ask "why will this set of outputs lead to this set of outcomes?" Asking this question can help identify assumptions about your program and its intended impact and lead to smarter and more effective program design and implementation. More on specifying, measuring, and evaluating outputs and outcomes is provided below in step 5.

Inputs

Leigh and Blakely identify five types of resources that are necessary inputs for successful economic development. These five Ms are Materials, (hu)Man Power, Management, Markets, and Money (Table 3). Fortunately, our assessment process above will have already identified many of these assets that are available to apply to CED. The goal here is to clarify which assets/resources are needed and how these will be utilized specifically to achieve your CED outputs and outcomes. Note that there are two levels to consider, the first being your specific project and what will be required to successfully develop, launch, and operate your CED program. Extending our example of a business incubator program, necessary inputs may include: the type of space required and preferred location to hold classes and sessions (materials); trainers, coaches, and other personnel (human power); demand for business-incubation services, communication and recruitment strategy (markets); leadership, partnership development (management); and funds required to launch, pathway to a sustainable-revenue model (money). These inputs are examples of what you will need in order to produce or deliver the *outputs* of your program.

---

24. For a useful guide, see Kellog Foundation, *Logic Model Development Guide.*

TABLE 3: THE FIVE MS FOR ECONOMIC DEVELOPMENT[25]

Materials	Land
	Buildings
	Location
	Infrastructure/natural resources
(Hu)Man Power	Skilled personnel
	Available workforce
	Education and training capacity
Markets	Markets analysis
	Competition
	Penetration
	Marketing Strategy
Management	Organizational structure
	Managers/operators
	Research and development
	Marketing and sales
	Legal
Money	Equity/ownership capital
	Debt/borrowed funds
	Capitalizing institutions
	Subsidy and substitutes for direct capital

The second level of consideration for inputs is at the community level, looking at *outcomes*. For example, if your desired outcome is "successful small businesses with five or more employees," what inputs will these businesses need to launch and thrive? As an example, they will need space and a location conducive to local commerce (materials); an available workforce with the right skills (human power); a business strategy incorporating consumer demand, competition, reaching customers (markets); specialized support for legal, human resources, sales (management); and start-up and growth capital (money). As you design and implement your CED strategy, accounting for this second level of inputs will help ensure that your program successfully moves from simply generating outputs to realizing the outcomes that are the ultimate goal of your CED strategy. This discussion

25. From Leigh and Blakely, *Planning Local Economic Development*, 224.

also highlights the importance of having business, legal, and finance expertise on your core and advisory teams to ensure that both the outputs and outcomes have the necessary inputs and organizational structure to be delivered.

Step 5: Evaluation and Adaptation

While it may seem premature to think about evaluation before your CED strategy is even launched, it should be built into your program from the ground up in order to be most effective. In addition to contributing to solid program design and implementation, a strong evaluation plan is often required by funders who want to understand exactly what their grant or loan will accomplish and how it will be measured. Evaluation should also operate as a tracking and monitoring system to provide early warning if a program is not working as intended, and it can also keep your team focused on the essentials for program success.

Key to effective evaluation is a clear articulation of your objectives, which as we have described in the previous section can be thought of in terms of *outputs* and *outcomes*. Outputs and outcomes must be measurable and should be articulated in the form of progress indicators with specific goals by a specific date. While much has been written about establishing SMART goals,[26] what may not be so obvious is the need for data tracking and collection systems to support such goal setting. For example, if you wish to report on the business success of graduates from your business incubator program, how will you gather this data? Table 4 below illuminates the distinction between generic outputs and outcomes, progress indicators, and goals. It also includes a column to indicate the source of data for the progress indicator. We recommend developing such a table to guide your evaluation efforts prior to actually launching your program. Doing so will not only ensure an effective evaluation effort, but it can also aid in program design and implementation (step 4) by clarifying the critical aspects of your program in terms of specific outputs and outcomes.

26. See Eby, "Essential Guide to Writing SMART Goals," if needed.

TABLE 4: SAMPLE EVALUATION AND DATA COLLECTION PLAN

	Progress Indicators	Goals	Data Source
Program Outputs			
Program graduates	Number of minority graduates from Program	15 minority graduates by Sept 1, 2022 50 (cumulative) minority graduates by Sept 1, 2025	Program registration and participant database
Entrepreneur curriculum	Curriculum finalized and approved for use by board	Curriculum finalized and approved by Dec 31, 2022 Curriculum 2.0 finalized and approved by Dec 31, 2024	Management report
Program Outcomes			
Successfully launched businesses by program graduates	Graduate-launched businesses achieve first revenue Graduate-launched businesses hire first employee Graduate-launched businesses have 5+ employees	5 graduate-launched businesses achieve first revenue by Dec 31, 2022 5 graduate-launched businesses hire first employee by Dec 31, 2023 10 graduate-launched businesses have 5+ employees by Dec 31, 2025	Annual graduate survey

In addition to the data-driven approach to evaluation described above, you should also consider establishing a system to get broader feedback. Mihailo Temali suggests evaluating your CED program from four different perspectives: (1) residents and business owners from the community, (2) board, volunteers, partners, (3) funders, and (4) independent evaluation.[27] To receive feedback from the first perspective, residents and business

27. See Temali, *Community Economic Development Handbook,* ch. 3.

owners, periodic surveys or interviews should ask how visible and significant your CED efforts are to them and if they feel your organization is working in the best interests of the community. This also provides an opportunity to update your assessment work to gauge if new assets or needs have risen in the community, as well as solicit ideas for improvement. This perspective should also incorporate feedback from those directly involved in your CED program with questions on overall satisfaction as well as specific feedback and suggestions for improvement.

The second perspective—board, volunteers, partners—can provide a chance to go deeper with your questions, asking these invested stakeholders for an honest assessment of your CED efforts, their perspective on organizational health, and any changes they see in the community either in the form of opportunities or threats.

If you've established an evaluation and data-collection process as described above, you will be well positioned for the third perspective: funders. As your program and organization grow, it may also make sense to procure the services of a financial and administration expert who can analyze your budget, benchmark it with similar organizations or programs, and identify areas for improvement. Frankly, however, most small nonprofits and churches are on such tight budgets that looking for excess in their finances is laughable. Perhaps more critical is showing your funders prudence and good stewardship so that when additional staffing or other resources are called for, they will feel more comfortable supporting your new efforts.

Finally, the gold standard for evaluation is independent verification, captured in the fourth perspective. Firms that perform such evaluations will look at your outputs, outcomes, and data sources and evaluate them for clarity and credibility. They can also be asked to independently verify the outcomes in the community. In addition to such an "impact evaluation," you can also ask the evaluators to look at specific elements of your program, for example, program participant satisfaction or community awareness of your programs. As an objective source of information on your CED efforts, independent evaluations can be critical for those looking to raise additional capital from foundations or other granting organizations. Such evaluations also have the potential to uncover previously unknown or ignored elements of the program, providing valuable feedback on ways to improve productivity and effectiveness.

Adaptation

Rooting your CED approach in your church's vision and mission (step 1) will keep you going when doubts arise. Developing your program from a solid assessment (step 2) will provide confidence that you understand your community from both a resource and needs perspective. Choosing an approach as a CED strategy rather than an isolated project (step 3) will eliminate flailing from one project to another if changes in approach are required. Designing and implementing your program from a systems perspective with the end in mind (step 4) will help ensure that the right inputs and organizational elements are in place to lead to the expected outputs and outcomes. And finally, fearless evaluation (step 5) will keep you focused on what is most critical and can provide indications of where the program may need to change in order to meet the agreed-upon goals.

However, even after following the robust strategic-planning process laid out in this chapter, we can say without doubt that your program will not be perfect. Some programs may fail in their first implementation. While we do not recommend that you shortchange the process laid out in this chapter in the name of "starting small" or "failing fast," entering step 4 (implementation) with humility and a learning attitude will keep you from entrenchment. As mentioned in step 3 above, starting small with short-term impacts as opposed to going big and waiting for long-term outcomes is a wise strategy, conducive to learning and adaptation. We also recommend that the first implementation of your program be considered a pilot project with an emphasis on learning and gathering feedback. Such a posture will help you and your team be willing to change tactics and approaches, even while staying true to your vision/mission and overall CED objectives.

Program type	Offering organization(s)	Target population	Geographic scope	Notes on effectiveness
Microbusiness support				
Makerspaces and maker support				
Business incubators and entrepreneur support				
Worker cooperative support				
Mutually supporting local business networks				
Workforce development				
Commercial district revitalization				
Good jobs programs				
Faith-based affordable housing				
Community Land Trusts				
Anchor Institution programs				
Accountable Development advocates and interventions				

28. All worksheets shareable and adaptable, with attribution to David E. Kresta, PhD, under Creative Commons BY-SA3.0 license: https://creativecommons.org/licenses/by-sa/3.0/. Worksheets are available online at https://jesusonmainstreet.com/worksheets.

CED INDIVIDUALS AND ORGANIZATIONS
ASSESSMENT WORKSHEET 2

Individual or Organization	Individual roles: • Consultant • Enabler • Organizer • Participant	Organizational approach: • Development • Community organizing • Policy interventions	Program focus areas	Notes on effectiveness

Programs and Target Populations for Consideration			
Missing programs within your geographic focus area (as identified from Worksheet 1)	Target populations missing from programs	Church member expertise available to pursue program? Synergy with existing programs or partnerships? Ability to utilize church building or property?	Shortlist for further consideration (Y/N)?
Roles to Fulfill within CED Ecosystem			
You	Consultant? Enabler? Organizer? Participant?	What role and why? How will you (or team members) personally strengthen the CED ecosystem?	
Other team members			
Your church	Development? Community Organizing? Policy interventions?	What approach will your church take in CED? Why? How will your church strengthen the CED ecosystem?	
	Start an Economic Development nonprofit?	Why?	

Associations			
	Name of association and primary contact	Focus, purpose, activities	Potential fit and interest for CED efforts (business attraction, local business support, job training/placement, entrepreneur development, connectors, other)?
Minority/low-income groups			
Business groups			
Union/worker groups			
Hobby/craft/creative groups			
Neighborhood improvement, locality development groups			
Advocacy, activist groups			
Other			
Institutions			
	Name of institution and primary contact	Focus, purpose, activities	Potential fit and interest for CED efforts (funding, local purchasing, good jobs, credibility, leadership, connectors, other)?
Anchor institutions (hospitals, universities, museums)			
Nonprofits (CDCs, service providers, advocacy groups, economic development)			
Businesses (large, medium, and small, locally owned, women and minority-owned, industry clusters, local developers)			

Foundations and financial (regional, community, private foundations; credit unions; banks; local investor groups)			
Churches and faith communities			
Government agencies (economic development and community development agencies)			
Residents			
	Specific skills in business, legal, finance, economic development, other	Connections with associations and institutions	Employment, self-employment history. Interest/need for microbusiness, workforce development, or other CED programs?
Individuals involved in CED (from Assessment Worksheet 2)			
Minorities/immigrants			
Church members, attendees, program participants			
Community leaders, activists			
Informal leaders (Facebook, Nextdoor, etc)			
Faith leaders			
Members/participants in associations			
The unconnected			

Physical Space			
Create and attach map view			
	Address/cross streets Contact info for owners and/or primary occupants	Functions/ activities in this space	How does it currently contribute or detract from community thriving? How can it contribute to CED?
Major landmarks (large buildings, institutions, parks)			
Underutilized space (abandoned buildings, empty lots, parking lots)			
Transportation assets (bus stops, light rail, major thoroughfares, bike lanes, park&ride)			
Community hubs where people congregate (parks, third spaces, churches)			
Economic hubs (markets, shopping centers, commercial districts, restaurant clusters)			
Economic/Exchange			
See also businesses/anchors, economic hubs, CED ecosystem			
	Address/cross streets Contact info	Type of business, type of marketing/ community visibility?	Interest/need for microenterprise development, makerspace, or other CED support?
Street vendors (locations, clusters)			
Informal businesses			

CED INITIAL STRATEGY DECISION WORKSHEET 5

	Programs/target populations shortlisted for further consideration (from Worksheet 3)		
	Short description including target population	Comments/notes from evaluation below	Decision: Pursue now/ defer/reject?
Candidate program A:			
Candidate program B:			
Candidate program C:			
	Evaluation against tradeoffs and other criteria		
Meets visible, urgent community needs, addresses marginalized population, fills CED ecosystem gap	Yes/Strong OK/Medium No/Weak ⟵————————————⟶		Reference worksheets 3 and 4
Aligns with church assets (expertise, existing programs or partnerships, buildings/ property)	Yes/Strong OK/Medium No/Weak ⟵————————————⟶		Reference worksheets 3 and 4
Leverages community assets (ability to work with not for, partnership potential, institutional support, builds on physical and economic assets)	Yes/Strong OK/Medium No/Weak ⟵————————————⟶		Reference worksheet 4

Short-term economic impacts instead of big payoff in future	Yes (preferred) ⟷ No		Recommend initial focus on short-term impacts, utilizing existing CED ecosystem
Requires significant organizational/ ecosystem capacity building	Yes ⟷ No (preferred)		
Opportunistic (leverages planned major development, funder or grant interest)	Yes ⟷ No		Consider tradeoff with other criteria
Church can accomplish alone, or will require significant partnering?	Church only ⟷ Significant Partnering		Consider strength of existing partnerships, complexity of program, and longevity of a church-only approach
Promises impacts for general community or specific group?	General community impact ⟷ Focused impact		Consider in relation to mission for marginalized, amount of fragmentation in community
Highly visible, symbolic, catalytic potential?	Yes/Strong	OK/Medium ⟷	No/Weak	Ability to generate excitement and inspiration?
Project that can grow to fill a strategic CED role with additional projects, programs, partnerships,	Yes/Strong	OK/Medium ⟷	No/Weak	Consider potential for follow-on projects and synergy with other CED programs

14

Context-Sensitive CED

Overview

By DEFINITION, CED IS intimately tied to place, calling for flexibility and adaptation to the specifics of each locale to which it is applied. The assessment process described in the previous chapter will identify unique assets and needs in your community, but here we provide some important general considerations for specific types of communities to guide your CED strategies. Note that while we provide recommendations on priorities and approaches, these should not be considered prescriptive but rather suggestive, subject to the findings from your community assessment. This chapter will discuss opportunities and challenges for the following types of communities: (1) early and late-stage gentrified, (2) concentrated urban poverty, (3) poor suburban, and (4) affluent suburban.

Gentrified Communities

"Gentrification" is a term used to describe a particular type of neighborhood change in which low-income neighborhoods become attractive to highly educated, higher-income people. In the process, low-income residents are displaced, racial demographics transition to predominately white, home prices and rents increase dramatically, and existing businesses are replaced by businesses that cater to new residents. Amenities such as bike lanes and improved parks suddenly appear in these traditionally under-resourced communities, with long-time residents left to wonder why these improvements didn't occur twenty or thirty years ago. Sadly, even existing residents who have the economic means to stay in their homes often no longer feel at home in their gentrified neighborhoods.

Early-Stage Gentrification

Communities at the greatest risk of gentrification are typically close-in neighborhoods that have gone through a long period of decline and divestment, often accompanied by "white flight"[1] to the suburbs. However, with relatively low property values and vacant buildings, investors now see opportunity for significant financial returns by purchasing and renovating homes in these neighborhoods, attracting mostly white, affluent residents back to the city to escape the suburbs.

CED practitioners must be vigilant in neighborhoods at risk of early-stage gentrification, as rising home and rent prices will exert displacement pressures on current residents. Ensuring the protection of existing affordable housing, developing additional units, and establishing community land trusts (chapter 10) should all be seriously considered as defensive measures to keep the community for the existing residents.

Such neighborhoods offer unique opportunities for CED as well. For example, you can leverage the emerging interest in your neighborhood to fuel commercial district revitalization (chapter 8) and attract new businesses to provide more jobs for local residents. It is important to ensure that a significant percentage of new businesses target existing residents, however, avoiding "commercial gentrification" which can contribute to alienation of existing residents from their community. CED can provide special assistance to existing businesses owned by local residents to help them expand and/or upgrade their presence to be competitive with new businesses. The result is the ability to continue serving existing residents even as they benefit from increased revenues from new residents.

Finally, local governments often include these neighborhoods in their list of targets for TED programs such as transit improvements, business attraction, and tax-abatement programs to fund community improvement. Accountable-development interventions (chapter 12) are therefore likely to be required to leverage this influx of investment while protecting the interests of current residents.

1. Mass exodus of white residents to suburban neighborhoods.

Late-Stage Gentrification

Unfortunately, in most metropolitan areas there are many neighborhoods well into the latter stages of gentrification. These neighborhoods will have already lost a significant portion of their lower-income and minority residential base, and home prices will already be at or above median levels for the metropolitan area. Such gentrified communities will typically have a vibrant and growing economic base with new businesses and a steady influx of investment from developers.

Nevertheless, CED can still play a role to ensure that the economic opportunities generated by gentrification accrue to lower-income and marginalized populations. Community land trusts will be difficult to start at this stage because of high property values, but existing affordable housing must be protected and expanded to enable existing low-income residents to stay. Some progressive cities are going a step further and developing affordable housing for those who have *already* been displaced. For example, the Portland Community Reinvestment Initiative[2] is working with the city of Portland to develop one-thousand affordable housing units in the next ten years in the historically black Albina district. Although much of the black community has already been dispersed throughout Portland, the "Pathway 1000" initiative is designed to help rectify this through targeted homeownership and rental programs for displaced individuals.[3]

Obviously, keeping existing residents and helping displaced residents back to a community is only one piece of the puzzle. A robust CED program that works to connect residents to good jobs (chapter 9), along with workforce development (chapter 7), can help ensure that these residents actively participate in the now thriving community. CED can also encourage new business formation (chapter 5) and worker cooperative development (chapter 6) by lower-income residents and displaced residents. Such new ventures will have lower barriers to success given that the gentrified community is already on an upward economic trajectory with interested investors and increased buying power from new residents. While CED cannot turn around gentrification, it can help to mitigate some of its effects by tapping into the improved local economy with targeted CED programs.

2. See http://pcrihome.org/.
3. For more information, see "A new plan to combat displacement in N/NE Portland."

Concentrated Urban Poverty

While gentrification garners the headlines, the reality is that across America about twice as many neighborhoods experience decline compared to those that experience gentrification.[4] Pockets of concentrated poverty are not hard to find in most urban centers, with characteristics including high unemployment, low household incomes, a high percentage of renters, a concentration of people of color and immigrants, poorly maintained housing, vacant buildings, and shuttered businesses. While nearly all of the strategies outlined in this book will eventually be needed in such communities, CED efforts must be firmly rooted in the community and not simply thrown at residents "for their own good." If you or your church are relative newcomers to the community or are serving it from a church located in a different community, it is critical that you take on the posture of a listener and servant rather than a healer or savior. Establishing partnerships as the *junior* partner with long-standing churches and community organizations should be your first order of business. Even if you have been part of the community for a long time, following the assessment process outlined in chapter 13 is extremely important in order to identify as many community assets as possible from which to build your CED strategy.

Neighborhoods of concentrated poverty need hope, but they also need jobs. While focus is required, especially for new CED efforts, a dual-pronged strategy in poorer, urban neighborhoods can deliver both hope and jobs. For example, highly visible, catalyzing projects such as commercial-district beautification and other simple locality development efforts (chapter 10) should be considered for initial projects. Making such improvements a component of a larger commercial-district revitalization (CDR) project can build momentum and generate support that will be required to create significant, long-term change. In depressed neighborhoods, CDR may require concentrating efforts on a highly visible but abandoned or dilapidated commercial corner, purchasing or developing the property as described in chapter 8.

While CDR and locality development efforts can be symbolically and practically valuable for poor neighborhoods, generating and connecting residents to jobs, especially good jobs (chapter 9), must be pursued with equal fervor. Targeted, high-quality workforce-development programs (chapter 7) are critical to improve the economic prospects of residents.

4. Kresta, *Can Churches Change a Neighborhood?*

Given a likely shortage of employers in these communities, CED workforce development programs should expand the geographic scope of potential business partnerships to adjacent communities and other locales that may be easily reachable via public transportation.

Developing partnerships with nearby anchor institutions (chapter 11) should be seriously considered, as many of these are located near urban cores with mandates to positively impact surrounding communities. However, these institutions may struggle with practical ways to interact with those communities. Anchors should be asked to help fund CED programs, with requests more likely to succeed with specific CED plans rooted in a robust assessment and planning methodology. Specifically, workforce development programs should be crafted to connect local residents to jobs at the anchor institution. Anchor-institution partnerships can also strengthen locally rooted economies (chapter 6), leading to increased revenues for local businesses as well as increased employment opportunities through business expansion.

Poor Suburban

While poverty has historically been associated with the urban core, the reality is that since around 2001 more people in poverty live in the suburbs than live in urban neighborhoods. The "back to the city" movement of gentrification has further fueled this trend, with lower-income residents forced to the fringes of metropolitan areas in suburbs with cheaper land and housing. Suburbs are also becoming increasingly diverse, with many incoming immigrants moving directly to suburbs, skipping altogether the urban-core landing places of prior generations of immigrants.

Suburban poverty presents a number of unique challenges, several of which have direct implications for CED strategies. For example, most jobs in the suburbs are in service and retail, which as we've highlighted in our discussion on good jobs (chapter 9) are typically not able to support a family. Higher paying jobs are typically located in other areas of the city, requiring a reliable automobile or a long commute on sporadic public transportation. Finally, the invisibility of suburban poverty means that many existing community-development and poverty-alleviation efforts continue to target urban cores, with suburbs competing for funding sources that are committed to central city neighborhoods.

Most of the CED strategies for poor urban communities discussed above will apply to poor suburban communities, with some modifications. For example, suburban areas typically lack a well-defined commercial district, with dispersed strip malls that are usually not within convenient walking distance of residential areas. This "feature" of suburban planning makes it more difficult to find an obvious initial target for commercial district revitalization (CDR). To overcome this challenge, a more detailed demographic and economic analysis during the CED assessment process (chapter 13) may be required to find locations with the highest potential impact for CDR.

Workforce development programs (chapter 7) should play a significant role in poorer suburban communities, with a focus on connecting residents to good jobs (chapter 9). Such programs will need to incorporate provisions to help residents overcome transportation challenges in these typically automobile-oriented neighborhoods, with ride-sharing, carpools, and even automobile-purchase programs integrated into the offerings. Advocacy for improved public transportation may also be required to help connect residents to jobs without relying on a car.

Unlike their central-city counterparts, poor suburban communities may have fewer, if any, nearby anchor institutions. Regardless, telling the story of how years of neglect followed by gentrification-induced displacement has resulted in the migration of "their" community to the suburbs can help secure an anchor's commitment to a suburban community.

Fortunately, there is at least one asset class that suburban communities typically have the upper hand in: cheaper land, housing, and commercial property. This asset can make a number of CED programs more financially viable than would be the case in communities with less supply and higher prices. For example, large office or warehouse facilities that are vacant or underutilized could draw new employers to suburban locations. While business attraction is not typically a core component of CED, it can nonetheless provide powerful economic stimulus, but only if coupled with strong accountable-development practices (chapter 12) to ensure that current lower-income residents get preferred access to newly generated jobs. Cheap space can also be used to fuel programs such as makerspaces (chapter 4) that may require large amounts of space for shared fabrication facilities.

Affluent Suburban

Affluent suburban communities are predominantly white, with incomes well above the median, boasting each metropolitan area's best schools and highest property values. While not uniform, such communities are typically more conservative politically relative to the entire region. As the domain of the megachurch, these communities are often marked by commuter churches drawing from a wide geographic area. While such communities may not be direct recipients for the CED strategies discussed in this book, their churches can nonetheless positively impact CED in communities across the metropolitan area.[5]

The first order of business for churches in affluent suburbs is to cultivate a vision and mission rooted in justice as discussed in the introduction and chapter 13. The need for CED, as outlined in chapter 1, must be established, drawing particular attention to the systemic nature of economic inequality. While some church members may push back on our analysis of inequality as a product of traditional economic systems, CED's connections to business and the market, along with the promise of long-term, sustainable solutions to poverty, should be of great interest to even the most stalwart economic conservatives.

Once your church catches a vision for CED, you and your church will want to fully deploy and engage the bountiful resources of your church as quickly as possible. Perhaps surprisingly, we suggest that you *defer* strategic planning and asset assessment. On this journey, it will be important to squash paternalistic and colonial tendencies that will likely arise, recognizing that the challenges of impoverished or struggling communities are rooted in economic systems, not in the personal deficiencies of individuals that can be simply rooted out through teaching or "relationships." Another particularly insidious temptation for affluent suburban churches will be in the area of leadership. Assuming that your church will provide some level of funding for CED, there is often the implication of getting a seat at, or even controlling, the leadership table. Sadly, this often has racial aspects, with whites struggling to take the lead from people of color, even when those individuals are truly the experts in their community.[6]

---

5. Of course, there are cases where affluent communities have some lower-income housing in close proximity. In these cases, the protection of the affordable housing, along with workforce-development programs, will be needed.

6. See for example Barber, *Red, Brown, Yellow, Black, White.*

To aid in fighting against this, we strongly suggest that churches from affluent suburbs seek out and develop partnerships, as the *junior* partner, with churches and other organizations that are already working on CED within communities in need. By taking on the posture of a learner rather than a leader, you and your church can build your "street credentials" and truly learn from the community you hope to serve.

At some point, you may be asked to participate in a program or asked to help solve a challenge. Following are some ideas that may fit your church profile better than others, but in all cases, your direction should be provided by the churches and organizations that are embedded in the communities that are being served:

1. *Connections*: utilize connections and political clout of members to bolster accountable-development (chapter 12) efforts. It can be powerful for elected officials and business leaders to see widespread community support spanning racial, economic, and geographic boundaries.

2. *Mentors*: provide mentors and coaches for a variety of programs such as microbusiness support (chapter 3), business incubators (chapter 5), and workforce development (chapter 7).

3. *Funding*: your church can help raise funding for CED efforts, including monthly support within your church budget, as well as special funding asks of the congregation. In some cases, members may feel more comfortable offering donations for specific items for a CED program such as manufacturing equipment for a makerspace (chapter 4). As will be discussed in more detail in our chapter on financing CED (chapter 15), a variety of mechanisms can be established to fund CED with church involvement, including revolving loan funds and congregation-based credit unions.

4. *Space*: if your church is conveniently located to the community you are serving, you may be able to offer office or warehouse space for CED programs to utilize. Keep in mind, however, that even the best of spaces can be a mismatch if program participants struggle to get there, or in some cases, if they feel uncomfortable driving into "rich" neighborhoods. Again, take the lead from your embedded community partners to determine if this type of support is appropriate.

15

Financing CED

Overview

WE AGREE WITH LEIGH and Blakeley in distinguishing between a *funding* and a *financing* mindset[1] for CED. Many nonprofits and government agencies think in terms of the former, emphasizing the ongoing collection of funds to pay for program service delivery. Financing, on the other hand, looks at opportunities in terms of capital streams, with initial financing necessary to implement a project, and flows of capital eventually building to a breakeven point where the project can pay back investors and generate cash flow to maintain and even expand operations. Accessing and layering these various capital streams into a sustainable financial model is part art and part science, often requiring engagement with consultants and advisors with specific tax, legal, and financial expertise. What follows is a very brief overview of the landscape for financing CED, along with this legal disclaimer: *nothing in this book should be construed as legal or financial advice; all decisions should only be made after seeking appropriate professional advice.*

There are two layers to consider in financing CED: (1) financing the organization delivering the CED programs, and (2) ensuring adequate financing for community members to start or expand businesses, perform locality development projects, develop affordable housing, or fund community land trusts. The focus for this chapter will be on the latter, although

---

1. Leigh and Blakely, *Planning Local Economic Development*, 226.

some of the discussion will also help you with developing a financial model for your CED programs and organization.

Below we consider a variety of financial actors as they relate to CED: (1) private firms providing debt or equity financing, with an expected payback or rate of return, (2) private entities providing grants with no expectation to be paid back, and (3) governments with taxing and tax-abatement authority. A fourth actor can also play an important role in financing CED: you and your church!

Debt and Equity Financing

Local banks and credit unions are typically the primary source of debt financing for individuals as well as business owners, but unfortunately these institutions do not always fulfill their mandates to provide for the financing needs of their communities, especially for minority-owned businesses and low-income individuals. Based on your community assessment, if you determine that a lack of accessible banking is a significant issue in your community, you may consider starting your own special form of a credit union, known as a community development credit union (CDCU). Inclusiv[2] is an organization devoted to helping communities, including churches, start their own CDCUs to serve low- and medium-income communities. Hope Credit Union Enterprise Corporation[3] is working to develop a network of church-led credit unions, something that may be of particular interest to more affluent churches. Although establishing a CDCU in your community will require significant amounts of startup capital and specialized expertise, it is a high-leverage activity that will maximize the impact of CED efforts, particularly those focused on business creation and expansion. Such an offering will also contribute to the overall vitality of the community, providing much-needed capital to residents for home purchasing, maintenance, and other expenditures requiring financing.

Equity financing is available from local investors, particularly social-impact investors[4] looking for attractive financial investments paired with local community benefit. Most metropolitan areas have groups of investors who meet periodically to consider new investment opportunities, often with a preference to invest locally. In addition to being potential sources

2. See https://www.inclusiv.org/.
3. See https://hopecu.org/.
4. For example, see https://socialcapitalmarkets.net/.

of capital for CED program participants who are launching or expanding businesses, social-impact investors may be interested in funding your CED efforts, either to launch a new program or build capacity to further serve your community. These local investors can also be invaluable advisors or board members to help guide your CED program design, providing an investor-perspective on what is required to launch and sustain a successful business.

Rounding out the first type of financial actor are private developers who may engage in public-private partnerships (PPP) for large municipal development projects, providing upfront funding for financial returns over long periods of time. PPPs are traditionally the domain of TED and often require accountable-development interventions (chapter 12) to ensure that adequate benefits accrue to the community. Further, as described in the appendix, private developers can play a role in smaller projects to redevelop church buildings and property, providing capital to initiate and complete church-based CED projects in return for future revenue streams from the redeveloped property.

Grants

Grants are allocations of money awarded without requiring repayment. Grants play a dual role in CED as important sources of funding for your CED program as well as to provide funding for your program participants. Relationships with granting entities should be developed early in the CED planning process, incorporating their perspectives into your program design to simplify the process by which local businesses participating in your CED programs can apply for grants. While foundations, particularly community foundations, are the most obvious source for grants, they may also be available from corporations with a local footprint and anchor institutions (chapter 11) who are interested in making visible contributions to the local community.

Social Venture Partners International[5] is a network of over forty local affiliates dedicated to what they term "venture philanthropy," providing funds for nonprofits and community-oriented causes with grant-like investment. In addition to providing funding, local affiliates nurture a network of community-engaged philanthropists, drawing on their vast business and financial acumen to help applicants fine-tune their business plans

5. See https://www.socialventurepartners.org/.

and proposals to increase the likelihood of success and maximize positive community impact.

Governments

Government at federal, state, and local levels can also be a source of funds for CED projects, with the federal Community Development Block Grants (CDBG) program as the most prominent source. A variety of government programs are also typically available to fund small businesses, including the Small Business Administration (SBA) which acts as a clearinghouse to match lenders with small businesses. In some cases, local government can provide significant financial resources in the form of attractive leases on vacant land or abandoned buildings in exchange for development that benefits the community. As discussed in more depth in the appendix, churches can also participate in a similar way by repurposing their property for CED uses.

Finally, there are a whole host of economic development mechanisms, typically reserved for larger TED efforts, that can be tapped to fund certain types of CED. Taking advantage of mechanisms such as tax increment financing, business improvement districts, opportunity zones, and empowerment zones requires considerable technical and financial acumen, but are critical components of the overall CED ecosystem.[6]

Churches

While churches are not often viewed as a *source* of funds, they can nevertheless play vital roles in the financial structuring of CED efforts. For churches with endowments and other sizeable assets such as buildings and property, these assets should be considered for their potential use in loan funds or grant programs for commercial district revitalization (chapter 8), microbusiness (chapter 3), and business incubation (chapter 5) programs. Taking these assets out of the safe confines of bonds and mutual funds and into the community will likely require significant conversations with

6. See www.cdfa.net for education and technical assistance in the broad field of "development finance."

church and denominational leadership, and may even require changes to governance policies, but the impact on the community can be significant.[7]

Your CED program may be able to generate revenue streams in a variety of ways, such as rents from properties and buildings that you have developed, program participation fees, or business revenue from businesses that you have launched. This aspect of CED financing is particularly important in cases where church properties are being repurposed to include business and other revenue generating uses (see the appendix).

Even a church with minimal financial assets at the organizational level may be a conduit to a substantial source of CED funds through its network of attendees. Many church participants will be willing to contribute to CED programs that promise tangible and long-term positive community impact, including those directly run by the church or those run by partner organizations.

Finally, churches can participate in CED financing by helping small businesses and entrepreneurs navigate the complexities of financing programs. This aid is particularly important for immigrants and other marginalized communities who may need help: (1) finding appropriate sources of financing, (2) building confidence, and (3) pulling together the needed forms and documentation to apply. Having a trusted coach or mentor to walk alongside them could mean the difference between success and failure for a budding microentrepreneur launching a new business.

7. See Elsdon, *We Aren't Broke* for a book length discussion.

16

Conclusion

WHY SHOULD YOU AND your church pay attention to local economic justice with everything else going on in your community and in the world at large? After all, there is certainly no shortage of issues in which Christians may engage, including racist policies, justice/prison reform, multiple refugee crises, extreme political and cultural polarization, abortion, declining church attendance, and so forth. I cannot make the case for the relative importance of CED compared to any of these, nor do I think that is the right framing. A similar line of thinking questions why a church should focus on CED when the real need is for "spiritual work" such as evangelism and discipleship. Again, I will not be drawn into navigating this false dichotomy.[1]

Instead, let's consider a word picture that has been challenging me for the last several years as I've grappled with my own personal calling. Imagine God as the Great Conductor. He is creating music, so to speak, bringing together a variety of instruments and voices with wonderful and joyous harmonies along with discordant and painful melodies. Guided by this view of God, instead of taking a me-centered approach, let's consider a God-centered approach. A me-centered approach focuses on which instrument I'm supposed to play, how I can get better at that instrument, and how I sound alongside my neighboring musicians. Of course, I want to be the best instrumentalist for God, but in a me-centered approach, it is still about how *I* can be the best to fulfill *my* role. A God-centered approach, on the other hand, puts the focus on the song and the orchestra he is creating, realizing that even the best instrumentalist can wreck a performance by ignoring the conductor. A God-centered approach listens for the music, joins in,

---

1. See Paul Louis Metzger's introduction for more on this.

rejoices in the wholeness of the production, and entrusts the performance to God the Great Conductor.

As the body of Christ here on earth, I believe God is calling his church into *more* engagement with our communities, and rather than detracting from the "true mission" of the church, such engagement helps to fulfil it. Arguing against CED because other issues are deemed more important is like arguing against clarinets because violins are more important. God's song incorporates *all* the parts to bring healing and renewal to *all* of creation. Of course, in making this argument, I am not naïvely calling for all churches and Christians to get involved in every topic and issue of the day. God recruits both clarinets and violins, not just generic instrumentalists. The answer, however, is not an equally naïve single-issue engagement with our world. Such an approach does not recognize the holistic nature of God, man, and society. Engaging with your community on economic development will create robust, holistic connections incorporating many other community organizations, people, and issues. A final brief case study will bring this holistic approach into view.

Holistic Community Engagement: Church of the Messiah

Church of the Messiah,[2] located in the Islandview neighborhood on Detroit's east side, has taken holistic CED principles to heart, spawning a number of initiatives including affordable housing, workforce development, job placement for those returning from prison, a food pantry, community organizing, youth mentoring and leadership development, business incubation, and more. The church takes seriously a major theme of this book, namely, the necessity of a community ecosystem to drive long-term and sustainable community change. For example, Pastor Barry Randolph is on the board of many local organizations including the Center for Community-based Enterprise (C2BE),[3] a cooperative incubator. He is also a founding member of The Master's Plan,[4] focused on ecosystem development in communities across Detroit and across the world. Their vision serves well to paint a picture of holistic community engagement and ecosystem development that

2. See https://churchofthemessiahdetroit.org/. Also see Jackson, "A church-run business incubator grows its community's own solutions to poverty," for more information.

3. See https://c2be.org/.

4. See https://www.themastersplanglobal.org/.

refuses to accept a single-issue mindset and the binary of spiritual versus secular:

> The plan is to organize religious organizations in and around Detroit to build the kingdom of God on Earth by the people of God. The scripture used as the mission statement is 1 Corinthians 4:20. It reads "The kingdom of Heaven is not mere words it is a demonstration of power." . . . The overall strategy is to build strong community by the people in the community at the grassroots level. Through partnerships people learn how to start businesses, become land developers, build equitable technology and media, and create community coops. Following the Master's Plan, people in the community reinvent their communities themselves. Big business, big government, big developers are not the solution. The people themselves building our communities. The Master's Plan significantly lessens the chance of racial injustice, gentrification, displacement, and classism. The Master's Plan is a model that can be used in almost any community. This plan creates Righteous Communities to empower the people to their highest goals.[5]

Words of Encouragement and Caution

For those who have journeyed this far in the book, you may feel excited, overwhelmed, or some combination of the two. First, some words of encouragement:

1. *It can be done!* This book has provided numerous case studies, some small and limited in scope, others broad and complex. Take heart that while each community is unique, all of the paths laid out in this book have been trod.

2. *It's not just you and your church!* As highlighted throughout this book, CED requires an ecosystem approach. In fact, your church must *decenter* itself, ready to play small as well as large roles in activating a CED ecosystem in your community.

3. *It's God's song!* We started this book by highlighting God's love for just economies, rooted in his love for people and justice. Now we finish with a picture of God as the Great Conductor who desires above all to bring healing and renewal through the music he is creating. Your CED

---

5. See https://www.themastersplanglobal.org/announcements.

efforts can be an important part of that song in your community, but remember, it is still God's song.

Now some words of caution as we ask: What can CED realistically hope to accomplish in the face of global economic forces, widespread institutionalized racism, and a volatile political environment? Can churches really change a local economy, and even if they do, can local economies make a dent in these seemingly intractable issues?

1. *Isolated CED programs are a start but will ultimately be insufficient.* Throughout this book we've tried to be realistic about the challenges and limitations of specific CED programs, along with the importance of linking CED programs together for more impact. For example, a makerspace (chapter 4) will have limited impact without the support of services from a business incubator (chapter 5) to turn a love of craft into revenue and jobs. Similarly, partnerships with an anchor institution (chapter 11) will require the development of a strong, locally rooted economy (chapter 6) in order to have significant impacts. The need for synergistic programs such as these will require hard decisions as to where to focus first and also call for the development of strategic partnerships to leverage the work of other organizations.

2. *CED must be local but not isolated.* As discussed in chapter 1, the very definition of CED entails place-based program delivery. However, chapter 2 also highlighted the need for community organizing and policy/planning intervention to create lasting change. Taking on these roles or connecting to such organizations within your broader CED ecosystem recognizes the importance of engagement with the broader political economy. Also, our CED toolkit has been explicitly broad, including several tools that require engagement with forces outside of the neighborhood. For example, accountable development interventions (chapter 12) will bring CED face-to-face with economic development at the regional level. A good jobs focus (chapter 9) and workforce development (chapter 7) may entail engagement with state government and large corporations headquartered outside of your community. Finally, in many chapters we have included links to national organizations that provide training and support for specific CED programs. These connections not only serve to minimize the time required to start your local program, they will link your CED

efforts to similar efforts across the country, magnifying your voice to a national audience.

Getting Started

Congratulations, you've taken the first step on the pathway to realizing God's dream for justice and thriving within your community! Here we offer some specific next steps as you consider what CED looks like in your neighborhood and in your church context.

Pray, Listen, and Scheme with Others

We suggest that you connect with other church leaders, members of your own church, and other community actors interested in exploring church-initiated CED efforts. Pray together, listen to each other's dreams for economic justice, and start scheming about what some of the CED programs highlighted in this book could look like in your community.

Mission and Vision Work

Dig into step 1 from chapter 13 to establish your church's mission, vision, and values around justice and a holistic definition of the gospel. If you and your church members can't honestly say that a workforce development program, a makerspace, or working with a local anchor institution is *central* to the mission of your church and *necessary* to be a faithful community presence, I humbly submit that you still have some more work to do in this area.

Do the Assessment!

Step 2 from chapter 13 provides a very thorough assessment process to understand your community and your church. Don't skimp and speed your way through this, even, or especially, if you already think you know what CED path you should pursue. Following the process may not only surprise you with new insights and open up new possibilities for engagement, it will also jumpstart your efforts to fill out a robust CED ecosystem, something that is absolutely critical for successful CED efforts.

I can think of no better way to end this book than to focus on the Great Conductor. While the song that he is arranging may be mysterious to us now, with many sorrows and injustices as yet unresolved, we know that its great crescendo will mean healing and renewal for all things. May God give you ears to hear the music in your neighborhood as you contribute a beautiful CED melody to his song!

> Then I saw a "new heaven and a new earth," for the first heaven and the first earth had passed away, and there was no longer any sea. I saw the Holy City, the new Jerusalem, coming down out of heaven from God, prepared as a bride beautifully dressed for her husband. And I heard a loud voice from the throne saying, "Look! God's dwelling place is now among the people, and he will dwell with them. They will be his people, and God himself will be with them and be their God. 'He will wipe every tear from their eyes. There will be no more death' or mourning or crying or pain, for the old order of things has passed away." He who was seated on the throne said, "I am making everything new!" (Rev 21:1–5a)

Appendix

Reimagining Religious Spaces

Overview

"Reimagining Religious Spaces" (RRS) is the tentative name for an emerging field in which churches across the nation are re-examining their current use of building, property, and capital, desiring to use these assets to their fullest potential in serving God and their communities. The triggers for such reflection include churches facing imminent closure due to declining and aging attendance, those seeking supplemental revenue streams to maintain financial viability, as well as those revisioning their relationship with their surrounding community. Churches often control the most valuable assets in a community, and as we've seen throughout this book, communities could benefit greatly from churches willing to reimagine their space in service to community thriving. There are several lenses through which we may consider reimagined religious space:

1. *Community development*: How can the space engage with a wide variety of residents, providing avenues for an empowered and engaged community? Examples include space for service and support for the homeless, community event space, space for nonprofits, arts space, third space, and community hub/organizing space.

2. *Community economic development (CED)*: How can the space support the local economy, contributing to overall thriving and livability, particularly for the most vulnerable? Examples have been given

throughout this book, including providing space for small businesses, business incubators, makerspaces, and affordable housing.

3. *Sustainable financial model*: How can the space support an ongoing place for worship and spiritual presence, while recognizing the financial realities of maintaining buildings and property? Creative financial approaches with developers, brokers, renters, and funders are required to develop sustainable revenue streams for the reimagined space.

Challenges

There are four primary challenges to realize the full value and opportunity of RRS:

1. *No standard roadmaps or guides*: Churches need help to chart their way forward, recognizing their unique context while leveraging experience from the success and failure of others. A preliminary process is presented below, along with references for numerous examples and case studies, to aid churches considering this pathway.

2. *Lack of domain knowledge*: The educational and professional backgrounds of most church and denominational leaders does not equip them to navigate fields such as real estate development, land use regulations, economic development, affordable housing, financing, and more. This book is a small step towards filling this gap, but much more is needed.

3. *Complex, cross-sector collaboration required*: Research recognizes the importance of a connected ecosystem across traditionally siloed sectors for community thriving.[1] RRS will require complex, collaborative projects with multiple stakeholders rallied around the common good. The CED process presented throughout this book lays the groundwork for such a collaborative, multi-sector process.

4. *Difficulty connecting to financial capital*: Projects in this field are often smaller than traditional housing and commercial development projects, making them unattractive to standard sources of capital. Connections with social impact investors, foundations, banks, community credit unions, and other sources, must move beyond the *ad hoc* and

---

1. See for example Benner and Pastor, *Just Growth*.

be nurtured into sustainable sources of capital. While chapter 15 of this book touches on financing CED, much more work in this area is needed to accelerate and support the RRS field.[2]

Preliminary Process Guide

RRS is an emergent field with a wide variety of approaches and pathways for churches to consider, made all the more difficult without the benefit of a standard map with which to gauge progress and determine appropriate next steps. We present in Figure 2 a preliminary engagement model for churches and other stakeholders to use as they consider reimagining their church space.

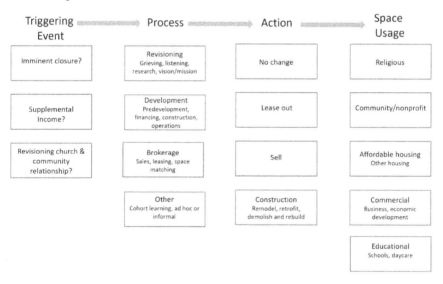

Figure 2: Preliminary engagement model for reimagining religious spaces

Triggering Event

Understanding your triggering event answers the *why* of RRS: Why are you considering repurposing your space? A preliminary situation analysis can set the parameters for the project, looking at current finances, attendance,

2. For example, see Faith + Finance at https://faithfinance.net/.

and organizational status, coupled with a desired end state. For example, if your triggering event is declining membership and likely closure within five years, are you hoping to maintain church ownership of the building with an ongoing physical footprint in the space or are you looking for a complete separation between your church and the space? If closure is not on the horizon, but the church cannot afford required maintenance, how much space can you repurpose and what type of new financial streams are required for a sustainable future? Or perhaps your triggering event is a desire to revitalize your church by increasing your church's investment and impact in the community, with a significant portion of the space repurposed for community uses. Depending on your triggering event(s), you should establish some overall objectives for the initiative, for example:

- "convert building to community uses, with 3,000 square feet of space for ongoing church activities"

- "generate $XXX upfront and $YYY of monthly rental income to cover costs for deferred and ongoing maintenance"

- "leave a legacy to the community, with the space becoming a vital community asset"

A realistic assessment at this stage can also establish the timeframe you have in which to work. Ideally, churches will start thinking about RRS well in advance of critical triggers such as imminent closure or an urgent financial crisis, driven instead by a proactive desire to bless their communities. Experienced denominational leaders indicate that most churches need three to seven years to work through the entire process successfully. Unfortunately, examples abound of desperate churches who have fallen prey to unscrupulous developers, resulting in grossly unfair financial transactions and property reuse not in line with the church's vision and mission.

Process

Because this is a preliminary process guide with roadmaps still being developed, below we provide an overview of the various types of processes that an RRS project may utilize.

Revisioning

Instead of immediately delving into discussions with developers or real estate brokers, churches should dedicate a substantial amount of time to "revisioning." Revisioning includes giving your congregation time and space to grieve, something particularly needed in churches with dwindling congregations facing the threat of closure. Many in your congregation may feel a sense of loss about what used to be and will need pastoral and community support to walk through this process. At the right time, the revisioning process can expand to start crafting a new narrative, moving from a story of loss to one of opportunity to bless the community.

Before deciding on exactly how you can bless your community, a thorough community assessment process should be followed. See chapter 13 for a CED-oriented assessment process that is built around an Asset-based Community Development model. The ideal RRS community assessment process will incorporate the CED lens provided in this book, along with a traditional community development lens that can provide a broader view of your community's assets and needs in terms of community empowerment and engagement beyond the economic.

The revisioning process is completed with the development of a mission and vision that grounds the entire RRS process in God's love of justice and people at the intersection of church and community. This book's discussion on mission and vision (see Introduction and chapter 13), while by no means complete, provides a good starting point. However, as a note of caution, the type of vision and mission called for here is perhaps different from typical exercises that are centered around the organization. Here, the vision is about the community, and the mission is focused on the intersection of your church, its assets, and the community. To aid in this orientation away from a church-centric view, we recommend that you create a mission and vision team that includes a number of stakeholders from your community, many of whom will have already been identified in your community assessment process.

Pre-development

Pre-development builds on the foundation of the revisioning process, creating several potential scenarios grounded in the assets, needs, and vision established during your community assessment. High-level financial projections are developed, along with potential funding mechanisms. Small-scale feasibility studies to determine viability of scenarios may also be pursued during this phase. In some cases, land use, zoning, and code issues may surface, requiring engagement with local governments to clear a pathway forward. Some pre-development vendors provide turnkey service with integrated development, while others may provide initial connections and discussions with vetted, mission-aligned developers.

Development

During this stage, developers are fully vetted and chosen, with requisite financial sources secured and legal agreements signed. The actual project size can vary widely, from minor maintenance and remodeling to complete teardown and rebuild. If your church will maintain ownership of the space, then provisions for ongoing operations of the repurposed space should also be planned and incorporated into the final project.

Brokerage

In most cases, the services of a real estate broker will be required at some point in the RRS journey. This can include selling the property or leasing space out after necessary construction has occurred. A particularly valuable service, space matching, can help churches identify community lessees who not only align with space and financial requirements, but also align with the church's mission and vision for usage of the space.

Other

Because of the emergent nature of RRS, processes will continue to unfold and evolve. One particularly promising engagement model gathers a cohort of likeminded churches in a community to explore RRS together. See below for a case study of a cohort model for churches interested in reuse for affordable housing.

Action

The specific action taken on a church building or property will of course be identified above. However, it is useful to call out potential actions at a high-level, as in this engagement model, to draw attention to the variety of choices available to churches considering RRS. In some cases, the right action is "no action for now," with a timeline for reconsideration. Some churches will choose to sell or lease space out, with little to no construction. In most cases, however, some level of construction will be incorporated into the development plans, from superficial remodels, to more substantial remodels, to complete demolition/reconstruction projects.

Space Usage

Finally, how will the reimagined space be used? Again, these uses will be identified during the RRS planning process, but calling them out at a high-level can help churches expand the horizon of possibilities under consideration. Categories of space usage include:

1. *Religious*: space for the current church or other churches.

2. *Community/nonprofit*: space for community hubs, social enterprises, and nonprofits.

3. *Affordable housing*: use of space for a variety of housing needs, especially affordable housing.

4. *Commercial*: space for CED programs, small businesses, and more, as described throughout this book.

5. *Educational*: space for daycare, private schools, public school homework, and tutoring space.

Case Studies

While affordable housing is getting the majority of attention for church property reuse, other examples include arts space, community hubs, entrepreneur and business incubation space, co-working space, lofts, breweries, childcare, fitness, and more. In most cases, the congregation seeks to ensure that the repurposed space contributes to community thriving and is aligned with congregational values, but this is not always realized. Some of these darker examples include luxury/loft housing which contributes to gentrification, lounges and nightclubs, and sadly, even strip clubs. Below are links to several collections of case studies showing the wide variety of uses that have been pursued:

- Performing arts partnerships in Detroit, Austin, and Baltimore.[3]

- Entrepreneur and business co-working space.[4]

- A large collection of case studies including lofts/housing, breweries, community centers, social enterprises. This includes "dark" uses such as nightclubs and strip clubs.[5]

- Affordable housing in Arlington, Virginia, including a space to rent back to the faith community.[6]

- Affordable housing case studies from across the country.[7]

- A large collection of case studies including affordable housing, arts, childcare, clothing, coffee/dining, fitness, health, horticulture, job training, recreation, and more.[8]

Highlighted Case Studies

Rockwood Center

In the winter of 2017, the Gresham and Rockwood United Methodist Churches in the Portland metropolitan area teamed up to convert the Rockwood UMC space into the Rockwood Center[9] where "Spiritualty and the Arts, Education and Opportunity, Culture and Community come together." The Rockwood Center provides space for microbusiness development, several educational ministries, community event space, and space for venue rentals.

3. http://sacredplaces.org/uploads/files/933961586160313874-creating-spaces.pdf.

4. See https://www.hawcreekcommons.com/ and https://themixcoworking.com/.

5. https://afterchurchatlas.org/tours/browse/.

6. https://faithandleadership.com/affordable-housing-rises-where-church-building-once-stood.

7. http://fw.to/gw8H7LB.

8. https://cbehnke.wixsite.com/maximizingmission.

9. https://therockwoodcenter.com/.

Portsmouth Union Church

In February 2015, St. Johns Community Church, a four-year-old church plant, was suddenly without a place to worship. University Park UMC, a church with over a century of ministry in North Portland but a dwindling congregation, offered space. The merged congregation, Portsmouth Union,[10] under the leadership of Rev. Julia Nielsen, has been on the forefront of a local movement to enable churches to build affordable housing on their property. The cohort-based Land & Housing Coalition[11] was launched in response to widespread interest from Portland's faith-community and the city of Portland to build affordable housing on church property. During this process, the city determined that over 600 acres of church land in the city across 435 properties is potentially available for affordable housing development. After five years of hard work, including zoning regulation changes and the creation of a city-faith community liaison to make these types of projects easier in the future, Portsmouth was awarded a $2.3M grant to begin development of a twenty-unit affordable housing complex on their property.

First Congregational UCC

Established in 1851, First Congregational[12] is a literal icon in Portland. Its beautiful building offers space for private and public events and notably houses the ArtReach Gallery. The church has long supported the arts, with exhibits documented as far back at 1875. ArtReach began in the 1970s, formally evolving into an art gallery in 2006. First Congregational's values of free expression, social justice, and ecumenicalism have been manifested in their use of space, blessing the community in the process.

Future Opportunities and Directions

COVID-19

The COVID-19 crisis will significantly alter the operating environment in this field for the foreseeable future. Aside from obvious disruptions to travel

10. https://portsmouthunionchurch.org/.

11. https://www.leaven.org/land-housing-organizing.

12. https://www.artreachgallery.org/history.

and business, church leaders are being called on to pivot to new modes of operation with significant disruptions to social and economic activity, both inside and outside of the church. As communities and churches emerge from this public health crisis, churches must be positioned to listen to and respond to needs for community (re)building and economic (re)building. We anticipate an uptick in RRS "trigger events" to reassess the current use of church assets in order to meet these community needs and address increased church financial struggles.

Joint Learning

As more churches consider and pursue RRS, it will become even more important to capture learnings from the field and share them out to a broad audience. This will help churches move much more quickly and effectively by providing guidance and direction from their peers as well as experts in the field. Potential formats include research-based field guides, online platforms for e-learning and collaboration, seminars, and cohort-based learning pods.

Church Preservation Trust and Clearinghouse

While supply of religious space is a critical component of the RRS field, equally important are the many community stakeholders looking for space. These community stakeholders include nonprofits, affordable housing developers, commercial developers, and other churches looking for space. However, metropolitan areas typically lack a systematic approach to matching of the available supply of religious spaces with demands that are aligned with the church's vision and mission. Local, online clearinghouses could provide such a matching mechanism. A more substantial endeavor would be to establish a trust that purchases church spaces and manages the portfolio to serve community demands for space.

Practitioner Directory

While RRS as a formal field is emerging, there are many experienced professionals who have spent literally decades helping churches and denominations manage their physical assets wisely. In addition, newcomers to the field are bringing invaluable experience and perspective from private development, financing, affordable housing, business consulting, legal, architecture, and other fields. Mechanisms such as an online directory to connect churches to experts in the field will be required to help churches move quickly and effectively as they consider RRS for their church.

Rethinking Seminary and Church Planting Curriculum

Finally, as mentioned in the discussion of challenges above, church and denominational leaders are typically not equipped to handle the myriad decisions and processes that RRS entails. Certainly, RRS provides an opportunity for leaders to draw on the expertise of their church attendees, and this must be encouraged and expanded. However, while church leaders should not be expected to be experts in far flung fields such as real estate, financing, affordable housing, or economic development, some basic level knowledge should be incorporated into their education and training in order to fully integrate church mission and vision with community thriving. Continuing to treat these as "secular" fields orthogonal to "spiritual" concerns will significantly slow down and limit the healing effects that the whole gospel can bring to whole people in whole communities.

Bibliography

Altman, Hilary, and Susan Rans. *Asset-Based Strategies for Faith Communities: A Community Building Workbook from the Asset-Based Community Development Institute.* Chicago: ACTA, 2002.

Anchor Institutions Task Force. *Journal on Anchor Institutions and Communities* 1 (2016). https://www.margainc.com/wp-content/uploads/2017/05/AITF_Journal_2016_Vol_1.pdf.

———. *Journal on Anchor Institutions and Communities* 2 (2019). https://www.margainc.com/wp-content/uploads/2019/05/AITF-Journal-2019.pdf.

Athey, Glenn. "Thinking about setting up a new business incubator or accelerator?" *My Local Economy,* February 3, 2015. https://mylocaleconomy.org/2015/02/03/best-practice-business-incubators-accelerators/.

Barber, Leroy. *Red, Brown, Yellow, Black, White, Who's More Precious in God's Sight.* New York: Jericho, 2014.

Benesh, Sean. *The New Cartographers: Helping Social Entrepreneurs Develop a Map for Church Planting + Local Church Ministry in the New Frontier.* Missional Challenge, 2019.

Benner, Chris, and Manuel Pastor. *Just Growth: Inclusion and Prosperity in America's Metropolitan Regions.* New York: Routledge, 2012.

Berner, Courtney, et al. *Successful Cooperative Ownership Transitions: Case Studies on the Conversion of Privately Held Businesses to Worker Cooperatives.* Madison: Center for Cooperatives, 2015.

Bigger Than You Think: The Economic Impact of Microbusiness in the United States. Washington, DC: Association for Enterprise Opportunity, 2013.

Block, Peter, Walter Brueggemann, and John McKnight. *An Other Kingdom.* New Jersey: Wiley, 2016.

Bolt, John. *Economic Shalom: A Reformed Primer on Faith, Work, and Human Flourishing.* Grand Rapids: Christian's Library, 2013.

Bretherton, Luke. "Religion and the Salvation of Urban Politics: Beyond Cooption, Competition and Commodification." In *Exploring the Postsecular,* edited by Arie Molendijk, Justin Beaumont, and Christoph Jedan, 207–21. Leiden: Brill, 2010.

Burke, Olivene, and Tarik Weekes. "The UWI Mona Campus positioned as an Anchor Institution: An Educational Perspective." *Journal on Anchor Institutions and Communities* 1 (2016) 11–20.

Cannon, Mae Elise, and Andrea Smith, eds. *Evangelical Theologies of Liberation and Justice.* Carol Stream: InterVarsity Academic, 2019.

Carpenter, Dick M., II. *Upwardly Mobile: Street Vending and the American Dream.* Arlington: Institute of Justice, 2015.

Casper-Futterman, Evan, and James Defilippis. "On Economic Democracy in Community Development." In *Entrepreneurial Neighbourhoods,* edited by Maarten van Ham et al., 179–202. Northampton: Edward Elgar, 2017.

Chapman, Jeff, and Jeff Thompson. "The Economic Impact of Local Living Wages." *Economic Policy Institute,* February 15, 2006. https://www.epi.org/publication/bp170/.

Chetty, Raj, and Nathaniel Hendren. "The Impacts of Neighborhoods on Intergenerational Mobility II: County-Level Estimates." *Quarterly Journal of Economics* 133.3 (August 2018) 1163–1228.

CityUnite. "A Place of Refuge." *Vimeo,* 3:30. June 14, 2016. https://vimeo.com/170676098.

Collier, Paul. *The Future of Capitalism: Facing the New Anxieties.* New York: Harper, 2018.

Crouch, Andy. *Culture Making: Recovering Our Creative Calling.* Downers Grove: InterVarsity, 2013.

"Data Shows Black Entrepreneurship Growing Across the United States." *Founder Institute,* February 22, 2020. https://fi.co/insight/black-entrepreneurship-is-growing-in-strength.

Davis, John Emmenus. *Starting a Community Land Trust: Organizational and Operational Choices.* Burlington, VT: Burlington Associates in Community Development, 2007.

Day, George. "Is It Real? Can We Win? Is It Worth Doing?: Managing Risk and Reward in an Innovation Portfolio." *Harvard Business Review,* December 2017. https://hbr.org/2007/12/is-it-real-can-we-win-is-it-worth-doing-managing-risk-and-reward-in-an-innovation-portfolio.

DeFilippis, James. *Unmaking Goliath: Community Control in the Face of Global Capital.* New York: Routledge, 2004.

DeYmaz, Mark. *Disruption: Repurposing the Church to Redeem the Community.* Nashville: Thomas Nelson, 2017.

———. *The Coming Revolution in Church Economics.* Grand Rapids: Baker, 2019.

Dimmick, Iris. "City Offers Help to Churches Seeking to Develop Affordable Housing Projects." *San Antonio Report,* November 13, 2019. https://sanantonioreport.org/city-offers-help-to-churches-seeking-to-develop-affordable-housing-projects/.

Building a Better Bay Area: Community Benefits Tools and Case Studies to Achieve Responsible Development. Oakland: East Bay Alliance for a Sustainable Economy, 2008.

Eby, Kate. "The Essential Guide to Writing SMART Goals." *Smartsheet,* January 9, 2019. https://www.smartsheet.com/blog/essential-guide-writing-smart-goals.

Elsdon, Mark. *We Aren't Broke: Uncovering Hidden Resources for Mission and Ministry.* Grand Rapids: Eerdmans, 2021.

Emerson, Michael O., and Christian Smith. *Divided by Faith: Evangelical Religion and the Problem of Race in America.* Oxford: Oxford University Press, 2001.

Eyster, Lauren, et al. *Understanding Local Workforce Systems.* Washington, DC: Urban Institute, 2016.

Frost, Michael, and Alan Hirsch. *The Shaping of Things To Come: Innovation and Mission for the 21st-Century Church.* Peabody: Hendrickson, 2003.

Garmise, Shari. "Building a Workforce Development System as an Economic Development Strategy: Lessons from US Programs." *Local Economy* 24.3 (2009) 211–23.

Giloth, Robert P. "Jobs, Wealth, or Place: The Faces of Community Economic Development." *Journal of Community Practice* 5.1–2 (1998) 11–27.

Heying, Charles. *Brew to Bikes: Portland's Artisan Economy.* Portland, OR: Ooligan, 2010.

Hirshberg, Peter, Dale Dougherty, and Marcia Kadanoff. *Maker City: A Practical Guide for Reinventing Our Cities.* San Francisco: Maker Media, 2017.

Holman, Will. "Makerspace: Towards a New Civic Infrastructure." *Places Journal,* November 2015. https://placesjournal.org/article/makerspace-towards-a-new-civic-infrastructure/.

Hoover, Melissa, and Hilary Abell. *The Cooperative Growth Ecosystem: Inclusive Economic Development in Action.* Oakland: Democracy at Work Institute, 2016.

Horsley, Richard. "You Shall Not Bow Down and Serve Them: Economic Justice in the Bible." *Interpretation: A Journal of Bible and Theology* 69 (2015) 415–31.

Hunsberger, George R. "Missional Vocation: Called and Sent to Represent the Reign of God." In *Missional Church: A Vision for the Sending of the Church in North America,* edited by Darrell L. Guder, 77–109. Grand Rapids: Eerdmans, 1998.

Imbroscio, D. "Shaming the Inside Game." *Urban Affairs Review* 42.2 (2006) 224.

Institute for Policy Research https://resources.depaul.edu/abcd-institute/publications/Documents/Workbooks/Asset-BasedStrategiesFaithCommunities.pdf.

Jackson, Angie. "A church-run business incubator grows its community's own solutions to poverty." *Faith & Leadership,* September 1, 2020. https://faithandleadership.com/church-run-business-incubator-grows-its-communitys-own-solutions-poverty.

Jackson, Kenneth. *Crabgrass Frontier: The Suburbanization of the United States.* Oxford: Oxford University Press, 1987.

Jacobsen, Eric O. *The Space Between: A Christian Engagement with the Built Environment.* Grand Rapids: Baker Academic, 2012.

Jacobus, Rick, and Maureen Hickey. *Commercial Revitalization Planning Guide: A Toolkit for Community Based Organizations.* Edited by Kate McDermott. New York: Commercial Market Advisory Service, 2007.

Jennings, Willie James. *The Christian Imagination: Theology and the Origins of Race.* Bloomsbury: Yale University Press, 2010.

Johnson, Neal, and Steve Rundle. "Distinctives and Challenges of Business as Mission." In *Business as Mission: From Impoverished to Empowered,* edited by Tom A. Steffen and Mike Barnett, 19–40. Pasadena: William Carey, 2006.

Kassoy, Andrew, Bart Houlahan, and Jay Coen Gilbert. "Impact Governance and Management: Fulfilling the Promise of Capitalism to Achieve a Shared and Durable Prosperity." *Brookings Institution,* July 1, 2016.

Kellog Foundation. *Logic Model Development Guide.* Battle Creek, MI: W. K. Kellog Foundation, 2004.

Kelly, Marjorie, et al. *Broad-Based Ownership Models as Tools for Job Creation and Community Development.* Takoma Park, MD: Democracy Collaborative, 2016.

Kenney, Andrew. "Denver Has a Housing Crisis." *Denverite,* May 10, 2018. https://denverite.com/2018/05/10/whos-got-whole-bunch-land-nothing-churches/.

Kresta, David E. "Can Churches Change a Neighborhood? A Census Tract, Multilevel Analysis of Churches and Neighborhood Change." PhD diss., Portland State University, 2019.

———. "Database Summaries." *Jesus on Main Street.* https://jesusonmainstreet.com/database-summaries/.

Bibliography

Kretzmann, John P., and John L. McKnight. *A Guide to Capacity Inventories: Mobilizing the Community Skills of Local Residents.* Chicago: ACTA, 1997.

———. *A Guide to Mapping Local Business Assets and Mobilizing Local Business Capacities.* Chicago: ACTA, 1996.

Leaven Community Land & Housing Coalition. *Discerning Whether Your Faith Community Should Build Affordable Housing: Process Guide and Technical Manual.* Creative Commons, 2016.

Leigh, Nancey, and Edward Blakely. *Planning Local Economic Development: Theory and Practice.* 5th ed. Thousand Oaks, CA: Sage, 2013.

Loh, Penn, and Boone Shear. "Solidarity Economy and Community Development: Emerging Cases in Three Massachusetts Cities." *Community Development* 46.3 (2015) 244–60.

Malizia, Emil, and Edward Feser. *Understanding Local Economic Development.* New Brunswick: Center for Urban Policy Research, 1999.

Mastrull, Diane. "Philadelphia Launches Push to Get Hospitals and Universities to Buy Local." *Philadelphia Inquirer,* November 26, 2018.

Metzger, Paul Louis. *Consuming Jesus: Beyond Race and Class Decisions in a Consumer Church.* Grand Rapids: Eerdmans, 2007.

"A new plan to combat displacement in N/NE Portland." *Portland.gov,* May 21, 2018. https://www.portland.gov/bps/news/2018/5/21/new-plan-combat-displacement-n-ne-portland.

"Overview: Worker Cooperatives." *Democracy Collaborative.* https://community-wealth.org/content/worker-cooperatives.

Parks, Virginia, and Dorian Warren. "The Politics and Practice of Economic Justice: Community Benefits Agreements as Tactic of the New Accountable Development Movement." *Journal of Community Practice* 17.1–2 (2009) 88–106.

Perkins, John M. *With Justice for All: A Strategy for Community Development.* Grand Rapids: Baker, 2011.

Reimagining Technical Assistance: Shifting the Support Landscape for Main Street. Washington, DC: Association for Enterprise Opportunity, 2016.

Rice, Solana. *Buy Newark: A Guide to Promoting Economic Inclusion through Local Purchasing.* Oakland: PolicyLink Institute, 2012.

Rothstein, Richard. *The Color of Law: A Forgotten History of How Our Government Segregated America.* New York: Liveright, 2017.

Ryzhonkov, Vasily. "Business Incubation Models." *Entrepreneurship, Business Incubation, Business Models, & Strategy Blog,* June 2014. https://worldbusinessincubation.wordpress.com/business-incubation-models/.

Salvatierra, Alexia, and Peter Heltzel. *Faith-Rooted Organizing: Mobilizing the Church in Service to the World.* Downers Grove: InterVarsity, 2014.

Schachtel, Marsha. *The East Baltimore Revitalization Initiative: A Commitment to Economic Inclusion.* Baltimore: Annie E. Casey Foundation, 2011.

Shook, Jill Suzanne, ed. *Making Housing Happen.* Eugene, OR: Cascade, 2012.

Sider, Ronald J. *Good News and Good Works: A Theology for the Whole Gospel.* Grand Rapids: Baker, 2006.

Sparks, Paul, et al. *The New Parish: How Neighborhood Churches Are Transforming Mission, Discipleship and Community.* Downers Grove: InterVarsity, 2014.

Stearns, Richard. *The Hole in Our Gospel: What Does God Expect of Us? The Answer That Changed My Life and Might Just Change the World.* Nashville: Thomas Nelson, 2010.

Stiglitz, Joseph. *The Price of Inequality*. London: Penguin, 2012.

Stone, Michael E. "Social Ownership." *Community Studies Faculty Publication Series* 7 (January 2006) 240–260.

Stott, John. *The Message of the Sermon on the Mount*. Downers Grove: InterVarsity, 2014.

Suttle, Tim. *An Evangelical Social Gospel?* Eugene, OR: Cascade, 2011.

Tannler, Nancy. "Removing Regulatory Barriers to Development." *The Southeast Examiner*, May 29, 2020. https://www.southeastexaminer.com/2020/05/removing-regulatory-barriers-to-development/.

Temali, Mihailo. *The Community Economic Development Handbook: Strategies and Tools to Revitalize Your Neighborhood*. St. Paul, MN: Fieldstone Alliance, 2002.

Tims, Dana. "Founder of Bob's Red Mill Natural Foods transfers business to employees." *The Oregonian*, February 17, 2010. https://www.oregonlive.com/clackamascounty/2010/02/bobs_red_mill_natural_foods_ro.html.

Ton, Zeynep. *The Good Jobs Strategy: How the Smartest Companies Invest in Employees to Lower Costs and Boost Profits*. New York: New Harvest, 2014.

———. "Raising Wages Is the Right Thing to Do, and Doesn't Have to Be Bad for Your Bottom Line." *Harvard Business Review*, April 18, 2019. https://hbr.org/2019/04/raising-wages-is-good-for-employees-and-doesnt-have-to-be-bad-for-your-bottom-line.

Turner, Nicol, John L. McKnight, and John P. Kretzmann. *A Guide to Mapping and Mobilizing the Associations in Local Neighborhoods*. Chicago: ACTA, 1999.

Voinea, Anca. "How has religious faith—or the lack of it—driven co-operative culture?" *Coop News*, August 4, 2019. https://www.thenews.coop/141134/sector/community/religious-faith-lack-driven-co-operative-culture/.

Wang, Elaine. *The Cleveland Evergreen Cooperatives: Building Community Wealth through Worker-Owned Businesses*. Washington, DC: Institute for Sustainable Communities, 2011.

Wytsma, Ken. *Pursuing Justice: The Call to Live and Die for Bigger Things*. Nashville: Thomas Nelson, 2013.

9 781725 275164